RAF Tanker
Navigator

RAF Tanker Navigator

Twenty Years of Air to Air Refuelling

Peter Bodle FRAeS and Tony Golds

Pen & Sword
AVIATION

First Published in Great Britain in 2008 by
Pen & Sword Aviation
an imprint of
Pen & Sword Books Ltd
47 Church Street, Barnsley, South Yorkshire S70 2AS

ISBN 978-1-84415-744-0

Typeset in 11/13pt Palatino by
Concept, Huddersfield

Printed and bound in England by
CPI UK

Pen & Sword Books Ltd incorporates the Imprints of Pen & Sword Aviation,
Pen & Sword Maritime, Pen & Sword Military, Wharncliffe Local History,
Pen & Sword Select, Pen & Sword Military Classics, Leo Cooper,
Remember When, Seaforth Publishing and Frontline Publishing.

For a complete list of Pen & Sword titles please contact
PEN & SWORD BOOKS LIMITED
47 Church Street, Barnsley, South Yorkshire, S70 2AS, England
E-mail: enquiries@pen-and-sword.co.uk
Website: www.pen-and-sword.co.uk

Contents

Introduction

In the spring of 2006 I was a happily retired ex-RAF officer who had settled down comfortably into a most acceptable rural retirement. Flying, working, defending the realm and all the other things we chaps in RAF aircrew were supposed to do, was well in the past – in fact over eighteen years in the past. It all changed when a colleague in my local lodge invited himself to Boughton for coffee, 'to chat about the RAF, air to air refuelling and that sort of thing,' he said. Little did I suspect that my comfortable, orderly life would be turned upside down, as this batch of recollections was extracted from my mind, cross-checked with log books, official records and the memories of colleagues who shared many of those experiences, and then committed to paper.

Air to air refuelling was the mainstay of my professional career, although training and learning one's trade, and constant re-training also took up a great deal of time and hard work. In the Canberra days, we had the youthful high spirits that permeated every facet of our lives. We happily roared over the tropical jungles at virtually zero feet, we partied hard most weekends and we took seriously our joint roles as defenders of the Empire and as God's gift to the world. We were arrogant, confident and impetuous, and in reality possessed all qualities needed to fulfil our roles.

Moving to tankers a few years later made us grow up extremely rapidly. We had the length of time to complete the course at the OCU (Operational Conversion Unit) and the Squadron acclimatisation training, to turn from young, fairly unregulated, testosterone-driven, bomber crews, into highly disciplined and responsible tanker crews at the cutting edge of air to air refuelling. I was assigned originally to the Valiant fleet, and although its demise was traumatic to us all, I have not dwelled on it at any length as it is covered elsewhere in several excellent books on the subject. Besides that, we tanker crews were soon urgently needed for the newly emerging Victor fleet, which would be the backbone of the UK's highly successful tanker fleet for decades.

Over the years I have had the privilege of visiting many countries and meeting with many famous and influential people, world leaders, royalty and members of foreign armed forces of all ranks. But even better than that, I have also had the honour of serving and flying with many superb pilots and aircrew, who I would number as being the best in the world, bar none. It would be churlish to miss out any of the superb aviators that I have shared the skies with, but it would be even more remiss not to mention some who influenced my life and career.

To all my fellow crewmembers and Squadron colleagues over the years, particularly the tanker boys, I owe a debt of gratitude for personal friendship and professional comradeship. Of the many, I do have to single out Gus Ross, Jeremy Price, 'Banfy' Banfield, and Peter Elliott to have a special mention, as they were with me at significant points of my flying career. Recalling memories of this nature, I can never leave out Ernie Wallis. He was an exceptional officer, an RAF legend and an unequalled expert in air to air refuelling. Probably because we were both navigators, me a Nav/Plotter and Ernie a Nav/Radar, I never flew with him. But I was very fortunate to have had him both as a chum with whom I shared many years of friendship and a professional colleague in an era when he showed all RAF navigators how the job should be done.

I hope this bank of memories that I have collected gives you a small insight to one of the lesser publicised areas of RAF flying excellence.

The views and opinions expressed throughout this book are those of the authors alone and do not necessarily reflect those of HMG, MoD, the RAF or any government agency.

Tony Golds
Boughton 2007

CHAPTER 1

Early Days

The red brick suburbia of the Golds' family home in Romford could not have been further removed from the country cottage of his grandmother where the young Tony Golds' first childhood memories started to form. Romford was a fairly typical smog-ridden 1930s London suburb and the Golds family was one of hundreds of thousands of hard working East London families who listened with increasing trepidation to the news of German rearmament, and the increasingly strident speeches for expansion and war from its leader, Adolf Hitler. Perhaps that is a slight exaggeration, in that it grabbed the attention of Frederick and Violet Golds, but had little effect on their three children, Jean, the eldest, Tony aged four and Doreen who was still a toddler. To them, life was mainly about friends, playing games and London Road School (Crowlands).

Number Two Stanford Close, was a typical mid-thirties, brick-built suburban family home tucked away at the end of a residential cul-de sac, not far from Romford town centre, its shops and the railway station. Like most houses of the time, it was a basic three-bedroom dwelling heated by coal fires and without the benefit of a separate bathroom, a hot-water system, or inside toilet.

The children and family washing shared the facilities of the kitchen sink. The children used it on a daily basis with the added supplement of a weekly (Friday) bath, and the family clothes wash

1

took it over on the Monday of each week. The water for all three activities was boiled up in a copper in the middle of the kitchen (until a boiler was installed over the sink by the landlord some years later). Violet Golds scrubbed the washing in the sink, on a ribbed scrubbing board. The table was then turned into a temporary base for the mangle, which she used for squeezing as much of the excess water from the washing as possible, before it was hung out in the garden on a clothesline to dry. Over the winter months an airer went up in the kitchen, as outside drying became a less than successful operation due to lack of sun and the effects of the dirt in the smog that hung over the whole of London and its suburbs for days on end.

The smog was a heavy sooty fog produced by all the coal fires that heated London's homes and powered its industry. This smog would produce the first childhood memories for Tony. At the age of three the smog and his father's lifelong enjoyment of some forty Player's cigarettes a day, conspired to give Tony a severe dose of bronchitis and a brief spell in the children's ward of the local hospital.

I can recall crying in the hospital, although at the time of course I had no idea of what was wrong with me. I recovered from this illness fairly rapidly, fortunately without any long-lasting effects. My life then followed the regular pattern for children in my area as I enrolled and began to attend London Road Primary School where my elder sister was already a pupil.

To her dismay, being several years older than me, she was compelled to take me to and from school on a daily basis. For this reason and perhaps others, I was not her favourite sibling and she was not afraid to let me know it. However, once at school, I did at least have a good bunch of friends to play with.

As time went on and the threat of war became a reality, we would often stand in the road and watch in awe as the planes in the sky wheeled and manoeuvred as the dogfights of the Battle of Britain took place over our heads. The noise of the German bombers passing overhead and the frequency of the heavy explosions of the nearby bomb blasts at night were as distressing to a bunch of five to six year olds as the aerial ballet above us during the day, was enjoyable.

Nonetheless, we were all totally convinced the whole show was put on for our very own personal entertainment.

Between the wars Frederick Golds had been brought up by his mother in the small, sleepy Sussex village of Horsham. Now, as the bombing intensified, he and Violet began to feel that it was all getting a bit too close for comfort, and as many houses in their area had been either destroyed or badly damaged, it was time to move the children away from the danger. Peaceful, rural Horsham seemed ideal. Thus in early 1940, Jean, Tony and Doreen were told by their father that they were going for a long holiday with Grandma Pyzer. Like so many other London children at that time, they were to become evacuees.

We said goodbye to Mummy as we climbed into the family Ford Eight and Daddy drove us to Grandma's. We had been there before so it was nothing new and Grandma Pyzer (Margaret) was a kindly, if severe, matriarch of the old school.

She was definitely from the 'children should be seen but not heard' brigade, but luckily for us was not that severe that we were frightened of her. Her husband (her second) Grandad Pyzer (William) was a quiet, hard-working old chap, who spent most of his time tending the rather large garden that provided us with a plentiful supply of vegetables and the once-a-week egg from the chickens they kept.

Grandma seemed to take the arrival of two young children and a toddler in her stride, and after the first night or two of tears for us, we settled into the routine of country life. It was boring and time dragged. Certainly, to a lively seven-year-old fresh from the war-torn city, it was deadly boring. In Romford I had twenty or thirty friends to play with, here I had three or four. I had lost my chums, my school, my toys, especially my cricket bat, but above all else I lost the war. It had completely vanished from my life. One day it was zooming about above my head on a regular basis and the next the skies were clear for what seemed like weeks on end. The nearest I got to the war in Sussex was to see the Italian prisoners-of-war walking from their camp across the road from Grandma's cottage, out to the fields where they were working. Even that was a let down, as they seemed a happy, smiling bunch of chaps, nothing like the scowling and fierce enemy soldiers we had imagined and talked about in our war games back in Romford.

The cottage the children lived in with their grandparents was a two-storey building with just two bedrooms upstairs, reached by what seemed, to them, a near-vertical set of stairs from the ground floor. The downstairs rooms housed the kitchen/living room and the front room, which had been converted into a small shop that sold everything: sweets, bread, eggs from the chicken and vegetables from the very large garden tended by Grandad Pyzer. Grandad Pyzer had a small hand cart that he pushed round the villages selling more of his home-grown produce. The young Tony was part of the selling operation, running back and forth between the cart and front doors to announce their arrival.

The Longhurst family lived almost opposite the cottage and fortunately for the eldest of the two Golds children, the Longhurst children (Sylvia, Teddy and Joyce) were of a similar age and attended the same school. It was on the long mile-and-a-half trek to and from school every day that the friendships grew and served to relieve the boredom of their enforced rural existence. To Tony, the village school was not anywhere near as exciting as London Road Primary and the elderly teacher, drafted in from her retirement for the duration of the war, could do little to spark the interest of a misplaced town boy. He was in a class of more than forty children who were at least a year below his class level at London Road. Most of his classmates were locals – very few were evacuees like him.

Exploring the local countryside was a favourite occupation for the children. They would spend hours on end dashing across large fields, wandering along meandering country lanes and farm tracks, and crossing the inevitable brook and stream, much to the detriment of their shoes, socks and particularly the young Tony's wellies! Jean was somewhat bigger and longer in the leg than her smaller brother and, as such, could comfortably stride across the streams and brooks that criss-crossed the local fields. It was on these occasions that he occasionally managed to fill his boots with fresh Sussex spring water. Grandma Pyzer failed to see the humour of the situation and somewhat unfairly it was Jean who received the telling off.

Although the evacuation had taken place in the car, from then on the deprivations of war demanded the use of the train service between Victoria Station and Horsham. For the next few years, the family Ford was taken off the road as the wartime petrol rationing bit into the motoring aspirations of the civilian population. Jean was old enough to pop back home on the train from time to time and their parents came to see them whenever they could afford it. But the disruption to the lives of the younger two children proved so disturbing that after two or three attempts, it was decided to cease the visits. In some ways this helped to hasten their return to Romford as the separation was so painful to Violet that as soon as the bombing eased back, Jean returned home permanently, and some six months later Tony and Doreen followed. Life for the Golds family in Stanford Close returned to normality, as far as it could, during the middle phase of World War Two.

I remember being dreadfully disappointed that the war in the skies above Romford had also disappeared in the eighteen months or so that I had been away. The Battle of Britain had been won. Any planes I saw were way above me and obviously heading elsewhere, as fast as they could go. However, there was still very much in Romford itself to recommend it to an eight-year-old. I was back home once more with Mummy and Daddy, I had my full selection of toys again and above all else I was back at London Road Primary amongst my chums. The school had smaller classes and a more disciplined approach to education with its crop of younger teachers. Unfortunately, none of these plus points re-lit the educational spark in me. For the rest of my academic career I would do just enough to get by and to keep out of trouble but not a jot more. A future for me in academia was not a likely prospect.

At this stage there was nothing on the horizon that could cloud my young life, or so I thought. But then I had not considered the next German weapon to appear in the sky over Romford, the doodlebug. As I found out much later, while I had been enduring my enforced stay in peaceful Sussex, the German scientists had been dreaming up and manufacturing the V1, later known to all British schoolchildren as the doodlebug. Initially doodlebugs had been great fun, especially when the RAF fighter boys started to evolve tactics that required them to roar all over the sky chasing the flying bombs. That, coupled with our own childish war games, involving the traditional small-boy noises of guns and explosions, fierce chases and hideously drawn out and over-acted death scenes, all added to a normal, enjoyable period of my life. Add to that Mummy's ability to produce fantastic dumplings, roly-poly puddings and other similar mouth-watering dishes and you can see I was pretty much a happy chap. However, the increasing attention of the doodlebugs and Mummy and Daddy's nervousness again conspired to re-acquaint me with the highways and by-ways of Sussex, and a further prolonged stay with Grandma and Grandad Pyzer. It also brought about a renewal of my friend-ship with Teddy and Sylvia Longhurst. Jean skipped this second stay in Sussex by being enrolled at Clarke's College in Romford to begin her secondary education. The return to Sussex also meant that once again the Romford gang of Tony, John, Derek, Geoff, Ian, Robert, Keith and Roy was broken up, this time until peace was declared and life could really return to normality.

The first days of that normality involved the return of the evacuees and a series of monster street parties for all the children in the area, which included cakes, sweets and all manner of delights previously denied the junior members of the Golds family for as long as their young minds could remember. In the run up to the end of the war, there had been a further addition to the family with the arrival of Delia. Tony was now the only boy in a family of four children. Only the fact that he was the second eldest gave him any comfort. He was still a nuisance in his sister Jean's eyes and a continuing target for her seniority complex. In her view her younger brother needed to be kept in his place, even if it meant the occasional clip round the ear to help remind him. The relationship normalised some time later, early in 1947, when on one occasion he retaliated with equal enthusiasm. After that the more level brother/sister playing field returned.

Delightfully for the children, one of the first things their parents thought necessary once the family was together again, was a holiday. The Devon coast was chosen and a two-week stay at Woolacombe was their parents' choice, squeezed into the short gap between VE day and VJ day. This was in fact to set a precedent for the Golds family and they returned year after year to the north Devon coast, sometimes to enjoy a camping holiday, but more often than not, to return to their first love, Woolacombe.

At the age of eleven I too went to Clarke's College and about the same time joined the Boys' Brigade. I enjoyed both, but my long established reluctance to shine at anything except sport, stayed with me all my days at school. I never really fell foul of the system and always seemed able to do just enough to get by and miss the wrath of my hard-working teachers. Clarke's was a co-ed school up to a point. Both boys and girls were housed on the same site, but strictly segregated. So much so that after chasing a well struck ball while playing cricket in the playground, I strayed across the line separating the girls and the boys. The ball was returned safely into play, but the error cost me a smart ruler across the knuckles the next day. (One stroke comprised both a downward stroke across the palm of the hand and an upward rap on the knuckles on the way up. That was always guaranteed to focus the recipient's attention.)

Having said that, I did of course benefit from two sets of friends, one group at school, the other at home. It was an ideal situation for a lively, athletic lad approaching his teens. Clarke's was also a good learning establishment, even if I did not take full advantage of it. Schoolteachers were returning en masse from military to civilian life, but even so we still had our share of older teachers, dragged from a comfortable retirement to cover during the war years. At Clarke's there was a Mr Barham, a retired headmaster. I was fortunate to have him as my form-master during the latter stages of my time at school. He was a kindly, patient man who worked stoically at introducing me to the understanding of mathematics. I suspect it was his vast experience in his chosen subject that enabled him to kindle in me an interest in that same subject, which served me well in later years and stayed with me throughout my service career.

School exams, then as now, tended to take place in May and June, just as the spring sunshine became established, and before the school caretaker got round to turning the heating down. Exams were therefore always conducted in hot, stuffy rooms, with the pupils occupying vast rows of single desks, all with large gaps between them in order to stop cheating. In the case of the pupils from Clarke's College, this examination hall was actually located remotely from the school, in a separate examination centre in Ilford, just a short bus ride away.

I remember leaving the examination centre with that now familiar, desperate sinking feeling that all had not gone too well. I was right, just two 'O' Levels, a GCE in Maths and another in Geography, were to be the sum total of achievements for my many years at school. Looking back it is impossible to see why later in life, others would see those two achievements as a satisfactory set of qualifications to start a career as an RAF navigator. That was however some way in the future. Before that, the brief interview with a chap dishing out careers from behind a desk on one of my last days at Clarke's, decided for me that I was to start gainful employment as a junior shipping clerk at the firm of Thomas Meadows Ltd, in Milk Street, in the City of London.

That being said, National Service was still very much the next real step after school for most lads of Tony's age. He and all his fellow juniors at Thomas Meadows were all very aware that they were marking time for a year or so until they received the buff envelope through the letterbox at home inviting them to become a member of Her Majesty's armed forces. Nonetheless, Thomas Meadows was a good place to learn the disciplines and habits of real work. There was the regular train up to London every day, the responsibility of even the most menial tasks, and of course the opportunity to grow up and learn to drink a pint of beer, smoke the odd cigar at the firm's Christmas dinner (one year held at the Savoy) and surreptitiously admire the rear end of the boss's secretary as she walked down the corridor! These were all essential rites of passage, for a normal seventeen-year-old lad.

Daddy and I chatted long and hard before the time approached when I was required to present myself for call-up. Radio and TV were the up and coming things – they were the future. So Daddy and

I hatched a cunning plan. I would volunteer for the RAF and take an apprenticeship in Radio and Allied trades, then after three years or so, Daddy would provide the funds for me to buy myself out. He would also secure the finance for me to set up a TV and radio shop in the Romford area and hey presto, my long-term future would be secured. It almost sounded too good to be true. It was.

I became a Corporal Apprentice and managed to reach the last five to be selected in a competition to be chosen for officer training at Cranwell. I didn't quite make it, but as my runner-up reward, I was selected to travel on a 'Round the Med' goodwill tour in an RAF Lincoln. For the best part of a month I had a high old time with the rest of the crew, showing the flag. We called in to many superb stop-off points that up till then had just been names on the school atlas, including Gibraltar, Malta, Cyprus, Jordan, Egypt and Kenya. We then returned via the same stops a couple of weeks later, before returning to the less exotic climate of Lincolnshire and RAF Hemswell.

However, after the passing out parade, the sunnier climes were still beckoning for Junior Adjutant Golds and a posting to RAF Idris near Tripoli, on the coast of Libya, was probably one of the nicer options for the start of his military career. During his short stay at Idris, the Squadron CO and his navigator took an aircraft from the line and disappeared off across the desert on a low-level practice sortie, never to be seen again. It was the first time Tony had been party to this sort of loss, but sadly it would not be the last. Indeed it would be the first of many such incidents, spread over the next thirty or so years, all involving RAF colleagues who would join the list of those chums and station associates who would not be coming back. Obviously the cessation of hostilities at the end of World War Two had not taken the risk out of military flying.

Shortly after arriving at Idris, letters from home started to indicate that all was not well with his father's health. In fact, each letter bore increasingly bad news and after a few short weeks the final message from home was the one he had been both expecting and dreading. His father had succumbed to what was in those days described as 'hardening of the arteries'. Today it is recognised that forty cigarettes a day for forty to fifty years, will almost certainly have a devastating effect on anyone's health and the length and quality of their life. In those days these things were simply not understood. Compassionate leave was of course immediately arranged and Tony was slotted on the first available aircraft home. It was the end of an era and in a way the final chapter of his childhood and growing up.

CHAPTER 2

Cranwell to Bassingbourn

It would be unrealistic to say that his future in the RAF was high on Tony's priority list when he returned home to share his family's grief at his father's funeral. It was, however, fairly high on the agenda when he returned to duty a few days later.

Plan A, to buy myself out and start a radio and TV business in Ilford had rapidly vanished into thin air. Plan B fell into place and I suddenly became aware that I could now look forward to a long stint in the Royal Air Force.

In the short time I had been in the RAF, I could hardly have failed to notice that the officers, even the most junior ones, had a much better quality of life than us mere mortals further down the military food chain. They had better quarters, a better Mess, better food, more money and prettier girls. There was nothing for it, I needed to become an officer, and quick! That required officer training, so I and my two 'O' Levels applied through the appropriate channels and to my great astonishment and delight I was accepted. I was soon asked to present myself at RAF Hornchurch to take part in the Officer Selection process. I have to say my Squadron CO provided great assistance to me in this endeavour, as he both endorsed my application, took me off all duties, kept me in the Sergeants' Mess and virtually force fed me a selection of books that would help to prepare me for my quest.

Officer Selection at Hornchurch seemed like hell on earth. On day one we were all subjected to a full medical, and I mean full. The Medical Officers were examining us in areas we didn't know we had and for things we didn't know we could get. Fortunately I did have what they were looking for and hadn't caught whatever it was I shouldn't have. So, on those grounds, I was declared physically fit enough to proceed to day two. This was all initiative and leadership tests; literally all the things you remember from the hilarious comedy films of the time, involving ropes, ladders, planks, poles and barrels. Day three was all about the selection of areas of career interest (mainly their interest in which path our career should follow. I was very conscious that we did not have an equal say in the matter). Day four was all about us preparing and giving presentations to our tutors and fellow students and about solving problems; in some ways I saw it as a sort of theoretical version of day two.

After all that Tony was sent home for what would become a regular part of his RAF career – Garden Leave. It was one of those uncertain periods in any serviceman's career when there was nothing that the RAF could do with them for the moment; they were away from their old unit and not yet certain of their next. Sending them home on leave seemed the best way of getting them out of everyone's hair until they were wanted for something else – whatever that was. In Tony's case his two 'O' Levels and a good selection report had worked – it was to be a sixteen-week stint at RAF Cirencester. At the age of twenty-one he had been given the go-ahead by their lordships to train for a commission in the RAF. He was to become an officer.

Plan B was now starting to show a bit more promise.

RAF Cirencester was home for officer recruits for a sixteen-week course in basics. There the new boys were given a rigorous dose of PE, Report Writing, Technical Presentations, Political Appraisals, Drill, Kit Presentation, RAF Law and yet more obstacle course assessment and training. All in all, they were put through the wringer for the full sixteen weeks. As fit as he was, Junior Officer Tony Golds still lost half a stone during those four months. Others without his sporting background and interests lost even more weight and a survival exercise for several days in the Brecon

Beacons certainly did not help those who were struggling with their fitness. Unsurprisingly, they were all as fit as they could be by the time they left for their specialised training courses. However, the fall-out rate was still high and only twenty-one of the forty-five that started the course emerged at the end of the sixteen weeks, to move on in their chosen careers.

RAF Topcliffe, just south of Thirsk in North Yorkshire, was to be my home for the next year or so as I trained to be a navigator at No.1 Air Navigation School. Shortly after our arrival, the tailors from Moss Bros arrived to measure us for our officers' uniforms and greatcoats. That, in our eyes, was the final seal of approval and another small step along the road toward my revised career objective. For we budding officers, RAF Topcliffe and its facilities had just what we were looking for; we felt we had arrived. Somehow, that was not quite how the RAF saw it and they had many courses planned for the cadets of the new intake to get their heads round, covering a wide series of academic subjects. For me, neither Maths nor Navigation were too hard, but RAF Law and some of the other subjects required a bit more concentration. We worked a five and a half day week, with Saturday morning being mainly devoted to parades and similar traditional RAF training activities.

We also had the start of our introduction to the social side of Air Force life. To no one's real surprise we all found this most acceptable and approached it with almost universal enthusiasm. We had monthly dining-in nights and the occasional dance, all of which I found extremely pleasant. I also now had adequate funds coming in to buy my first sports car, an MG TF. That, coupled with my recently acquired taste for smoking 'Passing Cloud' cigarettes and fairly frequent invitations to house parties in nearby Harrogate, had me convinced that I had really made it and had now found my real calling in life. It scarcely ever entered my head that I would eventually have to work for a living or that if I failed the course at any stage, I might well be re-coursed into Air Traffic Control (ATC), Fighter Control, or heaven forbid, the RAF Regiment. Such was the arrogance of youth that no such thoughts of failure were ever considered.

Although there was a great deal of theory and classwork for the budding navigators, the RAF system was to get them airborne as soon as possible. Therefore, on 11 January 1959 in the late afternoon, in groups of ten or so, they were shepherded aboard a Valetta for a quick trip around the local area. One hour and ten minutes later they were all back on the ground and writing their first entry in their newly issued Form 1767, Royal Air Force Aircrew Flying Log Book. Just over a week later, after a full and thorough week of classwork covering all aspects of basic navigation, on 20 January Tony and a couple of his fellow would-be navigators went up with an instructor in a Varsity. They spent the next two hours and ten minutes on their first real navigation exercise. They took it in turns to lie on their stomachs in the bomb aimer's position watching the world (mainly Yorkshire at this stage of their training), pass 2,000 to 3,000 feet underneath them as they sped over the countryside at about 150 mph.

Happily, I never recall getting really lost. Like all my colleagues on the course, I was occasionally 'temporarily unsure of my position', but never for long enough to cause a problem. I liked to kid myself that no one else in the plane had noticed my momentary lapses, but looking back, I'm sure that both the pilot and my instructor were well aware of the situation. After all, they flew this exercise on a regular basis and always with 'sprog' navigators, who by definition were liable to make all the beginner's errors. What they needed to see was how quickly we recognised our error and what we did to rectify the situation.

By February we were starting to have the exercises cranked up, and three-hour sorties became the order of the day. We continued to fly in pairs and alternated as 1st or 2nd Navigator as we started to learn our skills. By mid-February we were trying our hand at using the Gee kit [radar] on board. Then at the end of the month my last entry was an exercise of nearly four hours, which took my log book to thirty-one hours and forty-five minutes. We always plotted our routes beforehand and had a thorough de-brief after the exercise. I recall the de-brief lasted half an hour or so if you had flown a good sortie and anything up to an hour if you had not. Needless to say, we were all aiming for the half-hour scenario, even if it meant a

*longer time double-checking the pre-flight work a second or third
time before we took off. It was time well spent.*

The Varsity and Valetta were interchangeable during this part
of their training, although Tony's log book shows a somewhat
greater number of trips flown in the Varsity, and by the middle of
summer the magic 100 hours was noted in his log book. By then,
night flights were as commonplace as daytime exercises, as he and
his fellow trainees headed towards September and the final tests
and exercises that would signify the end of their basic navigation
training. Trips to Waddington, St Mawgan and Kinloss occupied
the first couple of weeks in September as they familiarised themselves with the arrival and departure procedures of other airfields,
and as they were introduced to the extra workload of completing
two sorties on the same day. Then for the final Navigation Flight
Test, they did a four-day round trip from Topcliffe to St Mawgan,
followed by St Mawgan to Gibraltar. There they had a day's rest
then flew a return sortie from Gibraltar to Lyneham and from
Lyneham to Topcliffe. The sector from Gibraltar to Lyneham was a
full six hours and forty minutes, the longest sortie they had flown
to date. Tony's log book was by now just a few minutes' short of
150 hours. The next month's section of the learning curve would
be on jets. They then went through the hypoxia, and spatial dis-
orientation training at Farnborough and then on to Plymouth for
the sea survival part of the pre-jet training.

Plymouth involved getting very wet and very cold in a variety
of differing, though equally unpleasant, scenarios. Initially they
were dunked in a controlled pool situation, then they were taken
out in the Solent in an MTB (Motor Torpedo Boat) and 'invited' to
jump out of the boat and wait around in the water (in the RAF
dingy supplied) and await an air or sea rescue. Although it was to
be repeated on a regular basis throughout Tony's service career,
this particular RAF activity never featured very high on his list of
'favourite things to do on a Wednesday afternoon'.

*Everything in my life at that stage was at full throttle. Pamela and
I had got married back in 1959 and she was now pregnant with
our first child. (While I was in training, there had been a group of*

us who met regularly and frequented the dance halls in Cleethorpes. Pamela and I hit it off at once and she attended many of the functions held during officer training.)

All of October was devoted to practising and refining all my recently acquired navigation skills, but at a much higher airspeed, as we transferred to the Gloucester Meteor. The dear old Valetta and Varsity had a maximum speed of between 250 and 260 mph, but the Meteor could gallop along at a close to a very respectable 600 mph; it took a few days to adjust to and gave us new boys in the navigator's seat very little time to admire the view. I flew on eight separate occasions in the Meteor before taking some leave and a month at RAF Lindholme on the Bombing Command Bombing School (BCBS) bombing course. It was while at Lindholme that 200 hours was penned into my rapidly filling log book. By then I had had six weeks to kill, between Lindholme and 231 OCU Bassingbourn and the mighty English Electric Canberra. More Garden Leave! During that time I was also unusually busy on the domestic front, as Pamela was having a really bad time with her pregnancy.

The Canberra was the ultimate state of the art, medium bomber in the RAF fleet at that time, so as fledgling crews, they could only stare lovingly at it during their first few months of the course. During that time they were rigorously put through their paces in ground school, on the basics of these superb new steeds. Fortunately they all managed to get through that part OK, due in no small measure to the earlier meticulous 'weeding–out' process of the well-proven RAF selection system. It was at this time that Tony met up with Monty Hall and Gus Ross who would shortly become his fellow crewmembers, but they weren't to know that until the last Friday afternoon of the ground course. Up until then there was a great deal of hard work to be done and a lot of partying to be had in the nearby town of Royston and the City of Cambridge. Not forgetting of course, for the big night out, London, which was just a mere hour away down the A1.

It was during this period that we met up on a regular basis with some of the Chelsea Set, who really knew how to enjoy them-selves. That was great fun. It was also at this time I cultivated my appreciation of really good food and wine, though I was still very much an enthusiastic partaker of Mess beer during the regular Mess and Unit functions.

As I said, it was at the final Mess gathering at the end of the ground course that we were all herded into the bar and told to sort ourselves out into crews. A couple of hours and a few more beers later we did just that. Gus [pilot], Monty [bomb aimer] and I became a Canberra crew. Now all we had to do was fly!

So, on Thursday 16 March 1961, Monty and I walked out across the apron in front of the hangars with our instructor F/Lt Mitchell, to Canberra T4 number 476, to start what would be, for me, a four-year relationship with the type. 476 was one of the training versions of the Canberra airframe and I was delighted that my first trip went like clockwork. In all honesty, most of the initial trips were mainly for Gus's benefit as he learnt how to fly the aircraft. My job was simply to navigate him to the areas where we carried out the exercises that brought him up to speed with his new mount, then steer him safely home.

That said, the instructors were doing this all the time, day in and day out, so it could have been argued that they hardly needed me, but it was all good practice. There was no room in a Canberra for four, so Monty was excused duties when we had an instructor on board.

It did not take me long to become familiar with the navigator's position, its layout and idiosyncrasies, and I soon became very conversant with my new 'office'. I was going to say comfortable, but that would be somewhat exaggerating. I soon realised why Canberra navigators were chaps of medium height and slim build. Tall or chubby chaps just wouldn't have fitted in the very modest space provided. Five days later and I was installed in a B2 bomber version and re-introduced to the idea of flying several sorties on the same day.

That Tuesday the Ross/Golds team flew one trip in the morning and a second in the afternoon. This was a pattern of multiple sorties that was to repeat itself many times over for the new crews during the next month or so, and included one day when they were scheduled to fly three. The take-off times spread from 1030 to

2130 hours, with the short middle trip taking place in the early evening. That was really a long day for both Tony and Gus, and for Monty who joined them on the last of the sorties when they were not carrying an instructor.

It was also during this time that they were actually learning to climb into and work in their new environment. This is not as simple as it first sounds. Obviously, Gus would do the walk round, chat to the ground crew if necessary and then sign the Form 700 that allowed him temporary custody of the aircraft. During that time, Tony and Monty would climb aboard, Tony first. He would throw his nav-bag in through the hatch, climb aboard and place both his bag and helmet (bone dome) onto Monty's seat and then scramble into his position behind the nav panel. He would then put his bone dome on, grab his nav-bag and strap himself in. It was then time to start setting out his kit, maps, flight regulations, 4A Navigation Computer, pencils and chinagraph crayons. In the meantime, Monty would have climbed aboard after him and also be strapping himself in and settling down in the bomb aimer's seat. Gus was last aboard and would also follow the same procedure, complete his cockpit checks and await engine start-up as the ground crew shut the hatch and did the final external checks.

By then I was in full work mode. You had to tighten the straps enough to hold you in place should you need to eject, but on the other hand, just a fraction too much made your legs tingle as you shut off some of the blood supply to them. I always tried to reach a happy compromise, which fortunately I never had to put to the test. On the training rig I would always strap up to maximum tightness, just in case. That was for a very short duration – I could live with that ... just!

I switched on the angle lights before the engines were fired up, as my workplace was a pretty dark, cramped area with virtually no natural light worth talking about. There was just a small window to my left about the size of a child's handkerchief.

I connected up my oxygen supply and glanced to the left and checked the bobble on the white and black indicator on my oxygen flow meter. My maps were already marked up for the day's exercise and in some cases a duplicate map was also prepared in case the first route was binned because of the weather or other outside factors. I had in my immediate possession the day's forecast and NOTAMs. (Notice to Airmen. This was the official way of notifying all pilots and aircrew of changes that might affect them – temporary closure of runways, changes of radio frequencies, air displays . . . that sort of thing.)

Monty and I could hear any chatter between Gus and the ground crew, so we had a good fix on the way things were progressing towards the take-off. Then several minutes into the sequence, the starter cartridge gave an almighty bang and the first engine would hopefully start up. A few seconds later there would be the second bang as number two engine was started and the whine of the jets built and stabilised as we prepared to taxi for take-off.

The operational procedures were identical for both the T4 training aircraft and for the B2 bomber variant. While on the course, the new crews swapped back and forth between both types on a weekly, if not daily, basis, and very occasionally would fly both types on the same day. The T4 exercises were mainly for Gus's benefit and the B2s mainly for Tony. Gus had the main differences in his department. The T4 had a single cartridge unit to start each engine; the B2 had a triple-cartridge system, thus allowing a plane with a reluctant engine to get the engines fired up without any additional input from the ground crew. According to the pilots, they all flew in a very similar way and certainly from Tony's point of view, both the navigator's stations were very much the same.

It was on 22 March 1961 that we all climbed on board as a full crew for the first time. It felt really good to be together and to be allowed to operate on our own. We were on a cross-country, so for once I was being fully put to work. It was great.

We came down to earth with a bump the next day when 728, the B2 we had been allocated, went 'U/S' [unserviceable] on us after just twenty minutes into the exercise and we had to return to Bassingbourn. Evidently something in the electrical department had gone AWOL. It was not super serious, but it reinforced in our minds the idea that all man-made things are capable of going wrong. It was all part of our learning curve.

These exercises were almost certainly a full ten-hour work shift for me. I usually started the route plotting on the map the day before the exercise and then added the wind and weather influencing factors the next day. The two-hour sortie came towards the end of a long work period, and only the de-brief followed. Half an hour after landing we were usually heading to the Mess. We always had to keep our maps and paperwork for a while after the flight, just in case there had been an infringement of any kind (low level . . . airspace incursion or other reported misdemeanour), that type of thing. Fortunately Gus and I never got into that sort of trouble, but it would have been easy enough to mess up like that if you did not keep your wits about you at all times.

On 14 April, the next new experience for Gus and Tony was night flying. F/Lt Green was their instructor for a two-hour session of take-offs and landings. The circuit bashing as it was and still is known, was mainly for Gus's benefit. On this trip Tony was just along for the ride. Once again, due to the seating situation, Monty was excused duties! The following evening it was the same again, this time with F/Lt Rickards in the instructor's seat. F/Lt Rickards was in fact the crew's allotted instructor, but due to the clashes of courses and leave, this was the first time they had an opportunity to meet up, some four months into the course. Of seventeen flights during the next month only four were daytime exercises. All the remainder were night flying exercises with take-off times between ten and eleven o'clock. The last for the month of May, and the last at 231 OCU Bassingbourn, was a flight of three hours and fifteen minutes with a take-off time of eleven o'clock. A week before that S/Ldr Moore had taken Gus and Tony up for their final check ride. Just two hours and ten minutes later they were back on the runway at Bassingbourn and were an RAF bomber crew in their own right.

There was a full passing out parade at the end of the course and the traditional big shindig in the Mess. We had already been told that

RAF Tengah (Singapore) was our destination and this was con-
firmed after the passing out parade.

Pamela was still having a bad time with her pregnancy so I
stayed at home playing the dutiful husband role, while lucky old Gus
and Monty took a six-week cruise out to Tengah aboard the luxury
Cunard liner, Canberra.

CHAPTER 3

Tengah and Canberras

Our son John was born fit and healthy on Sunday 18 July 1961. Having registered his birth, my next duty was to contact one of the MoD phone numbers I had been given, and advise the RAF that I was available to re-join my crew. I had already been down to London to be fitted for my KD (Khaki Drill) tropical kit, individually tailored by Moss Bros, so I was ready for the call the following week to fly out to meet up with Gus and Monty. Transport Command had one of their Britannias, or at least one seat in one of them, at my disposal for the twenty-three hour flight. We had a pretty brief stopover to refuel both the plane and its occupants; other than that it was non-stop. It was a long trip.

The first face-to-face meeting with the boys must have been really comical to watch. I was pure white from spending the majority of my time indoors in England with Pamela, while Gus and Monty were as brown as the traditional berries after weeks of lazy days soaking up the sun on a very pleasant extended cruise. My white legs sticking out from under my new Moss Bros shorts were a sure sign to anyone who saw them that I was the new boy in town, while the sun-tanned Gus and Monty blended in well with the natives. However, a liberal coating of iodine applied by my crewmates after a slightly over indulgent session in the Mess soon made a temporary change to the skin colour situation. We were allocated rooms in the Officers' Mess and quietly set about getting acclimatised to our job as guardians of one of the far flung corners of Her Majesty's Empire.

23

Full acclimatisation to the new role was not deemed complete by the powers that be, until a series of flights in the area had been undertaken, mainly to familiarise them with their immediate (500-mile radius) area. However, this was preceded by a rather unpleasant Jungle Survival Course at Changi, put on regularly for the benefit of newly arrived crews. The course was designed in two sections with the first week covering the basics of survival. First they were taught how to find drinking water, a seemingly plentiful commodity in a monsoon area, but one fraught with danger for the unwary. They needed water that did not give them stomach and bowel infections, and accessing that required detailed instruction on how and where to find it. So did the ability to catch and turn wild animals and insects into wholesome, if not enjoyable, nutritious food. With that being accomplished, they were then taught how to make shelters from the trees and local vegetation. It was all a far cry from the air-conditioned, gin and tonic laden, Officers' Mess they had left a day or so earlier. In addition to being taught how to cope with this basic unpleasant-ness, one of their Sergeant Instructors at Changi had a real conversation-stopping party piece. In a minute flat he would turn a live healthy rabbit hopping around on the desk, into a dead, skinned piece of nutritious meat ready for cooking – with just his bare teeth! It was a well-practised trick that was guaranteed to grab the attention of everyone in the room every time he demonstrated it.

After the Sergeant Instructor's rabbit trick, I remember adding a penknife to my personal checklist for all trips; Gus and Monty had similar thoughts. We had decided before the course started that we would stick together as a crew all through the two weeks and that seemed to work well for us. We noticed that some of the larger Shackleton crews split into smaller sub-groups and that did not seem to work half as well.

We were initially given all the dos and don'ts. Where to set up camp (on high ground not near rivers); how not to use the sun as a navigational aid (we were on the Equator); what was poisonous and what was not (generally the brighter the colour, the greater chance of it being poisonous); where to find water (avoiding the obvious big puddles and streams that looked clear and inviting, but were in reality crawling with stomach-churning bacteria). We were taught to catch fish, skin snakes and more importantly, crush and peel plants and flowers to extract safe, drinkable water. I'd like to say it was great fun – but it wasn't. We had already worked out that our chance of surviving a crash or bale-out over dense jungle was remote to the extreme. The jungle canopy was well over 100 feet high and the brilliant 'descent device' we were issued with as part of our kit worked well, but it did not have sufficient descent capability to get us to the ground if we unfortunately snagged at the very top of the trees. If, as we surmised, this was the most likely scenario, then letting go at thirty or forty feet was almost certain to lead to a matched pair of broken legs; not a healthy prospect for someone stranded a couple of hundred miles into a remote, hostile jungle.

The second week we had to put all this macho stuff into practice. We were driven out of the camp along a jungle track and at the appointed spot we were told to disembark and head into the dense jungle, where we were to make our first camp. We were to walk for a mile and a half to the north, turn west and walk for a further mile and a half, then south for a further mile and a half and then east for a mile and a half. That, in theory, should take us the whole week and eventually bring us back to our starting point. As well as living off the land, we had emergency ration packs and learned to cook chocolate, porridge and bully beef, sometimes all together and in the same pot!

Then it rained – oh boy, did it rain! That was another major talking point during the course. The rain at Bassingbourn and Lindholme had not been in the same league – mere showers and drizzle by comparison. Its ferocity and quantity gave us yet another reason to make sure we remembered to thoroughly check the aircraft before flight, not to accept any defects and attempt to get the aircraft home at all costs. We asked around when we got back and could find no record of survivors from any previous jungle crash. Our initial thoughts on crash survivability had probably been correct all along. When we eventually arrived back at our base camp, having walked right past it several times without identifying it until our instructor pointed it out to us, a light spotter plane dropped us a box of rations and life perked up for a while. But only for a short while. We then *had to head off to the Escape and Evasion section of the final day of the course.*

We swam across a sewage-infested river and marched, hobbled or crawled in whatever manner seemed appropriate, through villages and along tracks to the point where the RAF Regiment boys decided it was their turn to have fun and to capture us and put us through the interrogation section of our training. We were hosed down, roughed up, yelled at and generally intimidated into a state where we were supposed to talk. I have to say it was most realistic and extremely unpleasant. Then we were told it was all over and we would be heading back to Changi, where after a rest and some decent food, we would be taken back to Tengah. 'Oh and by the way could we please sign this MoD form to say you have not really been ill treated or abused?' I thought that this was a strange one and it threw me for a moment, so I refused. Later I learned that my instincts had been correct, as the paper had been folded so that in-between the regular RAF/MoD heading and the section for me to wearily scrawl my signature, there was a large enough space to write a detailed confession to cover a military take-over of the whole country! Lesson learned. We did of course then head back to Tengah, a bath, a shave and a good long session in the Mess.

Pamela and John had just flown in and so Tony was granted a couple of weeks' leave and used the time to move out of the Mess and into Married Quarters. To their delight they were allocated a superb colonial-style lodge in Singapore itself, complete with servants to run the place. He could now look forward to some semblance of normality into his life, and a long association with the social life of Singapore in general and RAF Tengah in particular. He also harmonised more with his son, though with an amah as one of the staff team, he was spared a lot of the more unpleasant and daunting aspects of the first phases of fatherhood.

Those two weeks soon passed and it was back to work. I seemed to recall our Squadron CO saying something like, 'orientate yourselves to this new environment, it's a bit different to that back home!' and by gosh he wasn't wrong. The Met man was suddenly giving me forecasts of thunderclouds (cumulonimbus – CBs) up to a height of

45,000 feet. What I failed to fully register from his briefing was that it could achieve that from a standing start in ten to fifteen minutes! I guess that having never experienced anything like that before, I just could not picture it fully. That rate of growth for a weather system was spectacular in anyone's book. The first couple of times it happened while we were airborne, Gus called us over the intercom and suggested that we poke our heads up front and take a look. It was truly awesome watching this bank of cloud growing in front of us at such an alarming rate. We did not, however, hang around too long to admire this handiwork of nature, and soon departed elsewhere to complete our familiarisation flights. Earlier, one New Zealand crew had failed to pay one of these beasts the full respect it deserved and neither they nor their plane were seen again. It was believed that the airframe was literally torn apart by the storm's ferocious internal currents and the debris and crew scattered many miles away over the jungle. It was a salutary reminder to us all that weather and weather briefings were a critical part of flying in that part of the world and one ignored them at one's peril. I have to say our Met boys and girls were superb. They were able to forecast the probability of these 'instant thunderstorms', or at least the weather conditions likely to spawn such monsters, with reasonable accuracy. It was a great help.

One other small weather constant at Tengah was the wind. It was either north-westerly, or south-easterly and, depending on the Monsoon season at the time, resulted in rain falling in the morning and sunshine in the afternoon or the complete reverse. Apart from a few very short periods, it rained virtually every day. The jet streams over the Equatorial area were more than a bit unpredictable. Again, our local Met boys seemed able to advise us with some accuracy when the jet streams were about to have a mind of their own and ignore their own operating conventions. Fortunately, although this was of great interest to Canberra crews it was not super critical, as we had more than adequate fuel duration and could always divert and escape the weather if we had to. I recall that just a few days later, one of the Squadron's B15s received a lightning strike whilst airborne, which put all the compasses out of commission. Needless to say, a quick radio call resulted in them receiving a QDM fix from base. (A radio call giving a heading for the pilot to steer to get the aircraft

to his destination airfield – usually in a straight line.) The heading
was constantly updated over the radio without reference to the on
board compass. (i.e. 'steer to port. OK now steer a fraction to star-
board. OK, hold it at that'.) This gave a comforting feeling to the
crew, knowing that they were in the capable hands of very competent
experts in the Air Traffic Centre. RAF Tengah was a very self-
sufficient air base; that far from the UK, it had to be.

The next phase of the training schedule belonged to Monty.
The bomb-aiming equipment, on the Canberra, although 'state of
the art', was still a mechanical device positioned in the nose,
from where Monty could peer knowingly at the two local practice
ranges at China Rock and Song-Song. This occupied most of the
months of August, September and October, with Gus, Monty and
Tony swapping between the B2 and the T4 like practised veterans,
although a break of a couple weeks was slotted in with some local
leave taken in September.

Tony and Monty also started to fly more often with other
pilots as Gus was occasionally seconded to other crews to add to
their experience. They were becoming fully fledged aircrew, and
Tony's log book was fast heading towards 300 hours. More of the
same type of exercises were to follow for the next few months as
Christmas approached. However, the pattern of bombing exercises
was broken by aircrew skill tests every six months, to check
that they were all up to speed and that no nasty habits had crept
into their flying routines. Then on 6 December they had an introduction into the art of formation flying under the guidance of F/Lt
Rivers. Half a dozen more bombing and cross-country exercises
followed over the next few days, then suddenly Christmas hit
Singapore.

At about this time, the New Zealand contingent went home and we
found our living accommodation was changed. We were allocated
ex-New Zealand aircrew quarters that were a cut above the average
for standard RAF hirelings. As it also came with its own amah
(Chinese), and gardener (Tamil), so the pattern of Singapore social
life soon returned to normal after just the briefest of diversions for
the move itself. As usual, our social life at that time was pretty much

party orientated. A few years earlier when I had the RAF career forced upon me, I tried to imagine what an RAF officer's life might be like. Now it was actually happening for me, I was not in the least disappointed. Each day was a joy and great fun – if only it could have carried on for ever.

Christmas was a period when it even exceeded my wildest expectations. There were Squadron parties and events; some with the ladies and some without. There were airmen's events to which we were invited, as well as the official Christmas 'do' at the Officers' Mess. The same occurred at the Sergeants' Mess and of course there was the Christmas Day tradition within the RAF, involving the officers serving the men their Christmas dinner. Coupled with all this there were literally dozens of house parties to choose from during the week or so up to 31 December. The Christmas parties only stopped when the New Year's ones started.

As well as fully enjoying all that the social life of RAF Tengah and the wider Singapore had to offer, Pamela and I also joined the current craze of buying a Mini Minor (red with a white roof) to drive around in and see the sights. In some ways this and the ability to stock up with good custom-made clothes and high-quality jewellery was meant to make up to the ladies for some of the undoubted hardships of life on the Malaysian peninsula. The heat, the humidity and the mosquitoes (the live sort, not the rather nice, but now obsolete, aircraft type) were all a nightmare to the majority of the wives the moment they stepped foot outside the protection of their air-conditioned homes.

Once back at work and with 1962 comfortably established in their log books, they began practising low-level operations. This was a different animal altogether to their 'normal' higher-altitude operations. Techniques practised for high-level navigation became a near impossibility and the majority of the Squadron navigators developed a system that combined some high-level navigation and some longer-distance horizontal, low-level navigation, using prominent and obvious landmarks as prime waypoints and markers for double-checking. However, the low-level exercises and sorties did allow a few non-regulation beat-ups of sampans and other small boats on the local rivers.

They also carried out a few more night training exercises, though mostly only when there was a full moon. These usually commenced once the semi-regulation evening thunderstorm over Tengah had abated. It was so predictable and reliable some aircrews claimed they could almost set their watches by it and adapt it as part of their pre-flight routine.

They flew to Hong Kong (Kai Tak) and to Clarke Air Force Base (AFB) in the Philippines to familiarise themselves with the operations of civil and other friendly Air Forces, not forgetting to take in a couple of days in Hong Kong along the way, to sample the more exotic night life and local colour. They also flew to the Australian bases Butterworth, near Penang, and Chiang Mai in Thailand a couple of times and spent some time with the Royal Australian Air Force and the ANZUK (Australia, New Zealand and United Kingdom) operation.

Some dive-bombing practice was required of us at about this time. I recall we transited to the bombing range at our usual 20,000 feet, then descended to about 1,500 feet to finalise the dive-bombing run, with me calling out the heights with a voice getting louder in volume and more urgent in tone as the ground approached. Starting with Don Muang, we also investigated a few of the more remote airfields in the local area, just to get some experience of these Second Division airstrips.

Rumour on the Squadron was rife in the late summer that we were to get some new kit, the Canberra B15, and sure enough, by October they had started to arrive and I soon had my first chance to get my hands on one. On 8 October, a Monday, I had two trips with Flying Officer Warren (Bunny) in 969, then two more in the same aircraft on Tuesday with Gus.

Five hours fifty, time on type, in two days was not bad going at all. I then had an air test with F/Lt Walker in 766, followed in quick succession by three more sorties with S/Ldr Leaske in 874 and two conversion flights for F/Lt Rickards and F/Lt Langdown in 969. By now Paddy Langdown, Monty and I had been given our orders to return 874, one of the older B2s, to England and return with a bright and shiny new B15. It seemed like a cracking good idea to me, and something a bit different from our normal flying routine. Whilst

*the B15s were in reality a mid-life upgrade of the familiar Canberra
airframe, they were totally refurbished inside and out and to the boys
at Tengah they could well have been brand new.*

The trip back to England had been planned in a series of fairly
short hops, usually of between an hour and a half and two and
a half hours. Even with an old B2 that meant they would have
no problem covering 800 or 900 miles in a straight line, which
would have given them fuel duration to spare. They had decided
on flying two legs of the journey each morning and getting all the
planning and authorisations for the following day's flights sorted
immediately they landed. This way the afternoons and evenings
were more or less left clear for relaxing, and as the flight unfolded,
it seemed to work well for them. They were also briefed to do all
their own after-flight servicing during the trip, and that was how
it played out, except for the stops in India, where the locals took it
upon themselves to help. Tengah to Minbu Airfield was the first
uneventful leg of two hours and forty minutes that took them away
from the Malaysian peninsula, and north into Burma, a distance of
close to 1,400 miles.

The aircraft was refuelled and Paddy gave it a quick once over
and they were off again, heading west into Indian airspace and
Dum Dum Airport near Calcutta. They had been on the ground
less than two hours and were soon climbing back to their transit
height of 30,000 feet.

*We coasted out some way south of Chittagong with the deep blue
of the Indian Ocean some six miles below us and headed towards
Calcutta and the vast Ganges Delta. After about half an hour Paddy
announced that its mudflats were starting to appear and for the next
half hour or more, even at our speed, the multiple mouths of the
Ganges and its thousands of square miles of silt islands and mudflats
passed below us. They were still there beneath us as we started our
descent towards Dum Dum and our first night's stopover.*

*The next day we completed the paperwork and the processing of
our flight plan to Delhi. It all seemed to be going pretty well until
just over half an hour into the flight, when I heard one of the engine's
whine change and slow down, coupled with Paddy's first Mayday*

call to Calcutta. Obviously there was a change of plan and we would not now be going to Delhi, at least for the moment. Calcutta ATC, for some reason, were not answering, and in-between attempts to raise them, Paddy advised Monty and me that the oil warning light on one engine had flickered and then stayed on, indicating that it was running out of oil. As it had been checked less than an hour earlier, it was pretty obvious we had a fairly serious leak on our hands.

After four or five further attempts to raise Calcutta ATC, Paddy gave up and asked me to find him another airfield. I rifled rapidly through my books and came up with Allahabad, a civilian airfield about three-quarters of an hour away, rather south of our planned track. They answered Paddy immediately and appeared to fully appreciate our problem. We were told to head towards them and call at ninety miles out and they would divert all other air traffic away from us. We were to expect a straight-in approach, and that is exactly what happened. After some rapid re-calculations I gave Paddy a fresh heading and we turned west-south-west towards Allahabad. I dug out the checklist for an in-flight engine shutdown, just to make sure Paddy had remembered to do everything that the book required. We had practised this before during our training sorties, so it came as no surprise that he had covered it all, despite it being a high adrenalin situation for us all, especially him.

Thirty to forty minutes later, out of my small vision panel, I could see the emergency services of Allahabad airport lined up along the runway awaiting our arrival. Comforting, but as it happened, totally unnecessary. Paddy did an exemplary asymmetric landing and we were directed to a hardstanding to park.

A Wing Commander of the Indian Air Force was there to greet us – a high honour indeed. He was charming and could not do enough for us. Amazingly, he then produced a Corporal Engineer with a wealth of experience on the Rolls-Royce Avon engine and an engine fitter with a box of tools who set about looking after 874 with enthusiasm. A faulty fitting oil-seal was proclaimed as the culprit, and incredibly, it was apparent that our Indian saviours also knew how and where to get the spares needed. Then our host not only announced that our presence was no longer required, but that he had also organised a car to take us to the hotel that he had arranged for our short stopover. He felt we would be more comfortable there and *anyway we would be on our way later in the afternoon. Paddy sent a signal to the Squadron at Tengah advising them of the slight change of plan due to the engine situation and I planned the revised route from Allahabad to Delhi.*

A couple of hours later a car arrived to take us back to the airport. The seal had been replaced, the oil replenished and the engine test-run to ensure that it had incurred no further damage. We never did get to see our charming Wing Commander again, but his Corporal and fitter explained that they had replaced the seal, made good the oil and carefully checked the compressor blades and inspected the remainder of the engine and were confident that it had come to no harm; obviously Paddy had completed the shutdown successfully before any damage could occur. They, or at least someone under their command, had also given the dear old Canberra a good wash down, so she was looking pretty spick and span as we waved goodbye to our saviours and taxied away from the apron to resume our journey. I'm sure the RAF received a bill in a buff envelope bearing an Indian stamp some time later for all this care and attention, but whatever it had cost, to us it was money well spent.

The run to Delhi was short, sixty-five minutes, and uneventful, though we were all very conscious of the engine note for the first fifteen or twenty minutes, and I also noticed that Paddy's panel scan was a little more attentive to the engine instruments than normal. Delhi was as hot and humid as we expected and the airport runway, taxiways and apron, as hot, dry and dusty as we had feared. The paperwork went through smoothly despite the earlier unplanned diversion from the published route. It never seemed to faze the admin boys in Air Traffic Control. Transiting British military planes were not uncommon and I just assumed that RAF paperwork still carried a reasonable weight of authority in those days.

Unfortunately, the iced water in the fridge in our rooms went through equally as smoothly. We had all drunk a welcoming glass or two and all three of us suffered with a minor dose of Delhi belly for the next twenty-four hours. I learned from that experience and from then on until the end of my flying career, I always drank bottled water when away from base. We were more apprehensive than ill by take-off time the next morning, so when we landed at Karachi we all headed rapidly to the airport facilities, just to make sure we were still on top of the situation. We repeated the team toilet trot some three hours later in Teheran, but by then we were all sufficiently recovered to enjoy the bar and the meals provided by our rather splendid hotel.

The route out of Teheran took them north over the Alburz and Talish Mountains. There was no room for complacency on this leg of the trip as they were too close to the Soviet Union for comfort. They had been briefed prior to take-off at Tengah that the radio beacons in that area were not always 100 per cent reliable due to the deliberate use of similar frequencies by Soviet anti-aircraft jamming systems. They had to be south of Armenia and north of Iraq and Syria and had a gap of less than 120 miles to use in the air corridor into Turkey. Passing over Lake Urmia was the route that gave them a half-hour transit over Turkish territory before coasting out south of the Taurus Mountains and into Europe. Once they were over the Mediterranean it was then only a short hop south of about 150 miles into Nicosia and the familiar sights, sounds and smells of a traditional RAF base. That was, however, only the first leg of the day, during which they covered the greatest mileage of the trip. Combining the times for both legs, 874 would have been airborne for exactly five hours and thirty minutes before it touched down that afternoon at the Luqa Airbase in Malta, on the completion of the second leg. They arrived at Lyneham mid-morning on Friday 2 November to a traditional cold, wet and overcast English autumn, a far cry from the weather on the first few legs of the journey. After handing 874 over to the ground crew at Lyneham, Tony headed off for a few days' leave with Pamela's parents in Cleethorpes, with the instruction to phone in on a daily basis to check when the B15 would be ready.

The following Tuesday that daily phone call confirmed that our plane would be ready for its acceptance air test the next day, so I re-packed my small travelling bag and headed off to Wroughton. At five past three on 7 November we lifted 208 off the runway – only to return it just thirty minutes later. All was not well with our new Canberra and the fitters needed a couple of days more to get things right.

We repeated the operation on the 9th and completed a further two hours of tests. We then had the weekend to kick our heels and it

*was in fact not until the following Tuesday that we were airborne
again. Once more 208 decided she was not yet ready for us and we
returned to Wroughton after just thirty minutes for another day of
fine-tuning by the fitters. Fortunately Wednesday's test flight proved
somewhat more successful and we were happy to accept the aircraft
and plan our return to Tengah.*

A flight just five minutes short of five hours saw them back in
Cyprus, this time at the more southerly base of Akrotiri. Following
a reciprocal route to the earlier outward journey and with night
stopovers in Cyprus, Teheran and Delhi, they arrived back at
Tengah with their new charge in the late afternoon of 18 November.
For Tony his next trip was with his Squadron Commanding Officer
in 667, a B2. The regular use of the bright, shiny and new Canberra
B15s would have to wait until the following month. Amazingly,
such were the patterns of RAF operations at the time, Tony would
not fly in 208 until late April the following year and would fly with
Paddy Langdown just one more time in the whole of his RAF
career, and that a month later on 22 May 1964.

However, it was now December and the 'old team' of Gus, Tony
and Monty was back together again. On 13 December there was a
short trip together. Then on 15 December Monty was given the
day off again as Gus and Tony headed off in 766 to the island of
Labuan, off the north coast of Borneo, with one of the Army top
brass (C in C, SAOC – Senior Army Officer Commanding) in the
spare seat. They stayed there overnight and brought him back to
Tengah the following day. Labuan was not the most comfortable
climate in the world, and the hardened aircrew of 766 could not
help but notice that it was a rather perspiration-soaked senior
officer who stepped out of the Canberra at the airfield, looking
somewhat less immaculate and distinguished than he would have
wished. The rest of the month was all about getting used to the
new B15s and their capabilities as a medium bomber.

It was their second Christmas in Singapore and the party season
lacked none of its sparkle. There were the usual RAF Tengah
functions and the more informal unofficial parties to attend and
'be seen at'. But there was an ongoing situation in the Malaysian
area with Communist insurgents and the team were back on board

a B15 for further practice, just two days later on 27 December. Fortunately, the take-off time was mid-afternoon, so someone had taken pity on them and at least allowed them a civilised start to the day, to get them back into the swing of things. They were airborne again on the 28th, the 31st and again on New Year's Day. It was a busy time. The first few days of January 1963 were all about bombing practice, high level and low level, with cross-country approaches. The bombing practice itself was at Song-Song with a regular load of 8 × 25-lb practice bombs.

The following week it was all change. We stayed with 766 and were assigned a goodwill, flag-flying, trip to Australia and New Zealand. We had a couple of long legs transiting out to the North Island of New Zealand where the prime object of the visit was an air display at the Royal New Zealand Air Force base of Ohakea. (We had completed a couple of practices at this, and Gus was fully briefed on the limits of his display.)

Leg one was 2,200 miles from Tengah to Darwin, with a flight time just five minutes' short of five hours. It was a long haul in anyone's book. It was also an unusual one, in that as we coasted out from Tengah, Gus set the throttles on the B15 and we just continued to climb to 45,000 feet until we levelled off. Then, at a little over nine miles up, he reset the throttles to cruise and we continued to climb gently as the fuel load diminished, to just over 55,000 feet. The feeling was totally unique. There was no one else at that height; we were on our own and the whole sky was ours. We were now ready for Australia.

After an overnight stop in the old town of Darwin we had the usual nine o'clock start on the next leg of the trip to RAAF Amberley, just outside Brisbane. It was another long flight with some 1,800 miles to cover before we touched down in Queensland. After our second overnight stop as guests of the Royal Australian Air Force, we headed south-east towards New Zealand and the RNZAF base of Ohakea. As with the previous day, we were airborne for three and a half hours including crossing the Tasman Sea and you can guess that the runway at RNZAF Ohakea was a most welcome sight.

While we were there, we were royally entertained and enjoyed the rest and relaxation that the Air Show provided. The boys at Ohakea included some who had recently been on detachment at Tengah, so we were back amongst old friends. They were a small squad, with just forty officers and 140 ground crew, but they had a fantastic rugby team that dominated the whole of that area – RAF, RAAF, RNZAF, British Army, and in fact anyone who cared to challenge them. They were a great bunch of guys to stay with and we enjoyed their company immensely. Sadly, time quickly passed and all too soon we had to retrace our steps and head back home.

We had, however, had the chance to go trout fishing at Lake Taupo, courtesy of our hosts, during some of our leisure time. So good was the fishing that we were soon throwing three-pound trout back as 'tiddlers', and not up to standard. We had quite a catch to repatriate to Tengah, and the Ohakea Mess fridge was pretty full by the time we were ready to leave. At each of the stopovers we rushed our precious cargo into the Mess kitchens and arranged for the Mess Sergeant to find a space for them in his cool room until take-off time the next day. For this alone we were treated as heroes when we arrived at Tengah on 24 January. The Tengah Mess Sergeant changed the menu later that afternoon to include fresh New Zealand trout! Not surprisingly, our period of fame was short lived and reality hit four days later as we were allocated a night air test in a very elderly and rather well used T4. Never mind, the New Zealand trip had been great fun and had added another twenty-three hours and five minutes to my log book.

February 1963 was a short flying month for Gus, Monty and Tony, but they did manage further training and practice in shallow dive-bombing techniques and a couple of low-level cross-country exercises with a very civilised lunch stopover. with the ANZUK team at RAAF Butterworth. F/Lt Whittaker was their instructor and he re-appeared on their second trip in March to check them out. They completed a few more bombing practice sorties and had their first real attempt at formation flying on 11 February.

March was also to contain another first. This time it was a goodwill trip, but on this occasion to visit the American Air Force at Kadena in Japan for Operation 'Joss Stick'. There would be a brief stopover in the Philippines at the enormous USAF air base at Clarke Field on the flight out and again on the return later the following week. Gus, Monty and Tony were allocated 209, the B15 Canberra they had used just a few days earlier for one of the bombing practices and for the formation flying exercise. 'Joss Stick' was to be a ten-day exercise in total, with a few days R&R, American style, thrown in for good measure.

They left Tengah just after eight o'clock in the morning and took three hours and twenty-five minutes to reach Clarke AFB. Later in the afternoon they headed north to Kadena AFB, just west of Okinawa City on the southern Japanese island of Okinawa. After the tropical climate of Tengah, the more benign climate of one of the most southern islands in the Japanese archipelago was immediately noticeable to the crew of 209 and greatly appreciated, as was the immediate move into the R&R section of the trip for the next few days. The bombing practice would have to wait. The Americans had it all planned and were going to do things their way and nothing would alter that. Not that they protested very much, you understand. They were heading to Osaka for a few days, on a 'get to know you', extended boys' weekend away. That seemed to include everyone: ground crews, aircrews and senior officers alike.

The accommodation was excellent, as was the food (especially the superb sea-food dishes), the hospitality and the entertainment, all laid on courtesy of the USAF. Such was their hosts' attention to detail, that at dinner they even had an ice sculpture of the Flying Camel logo of 45 Squadron adorning the centre of their table. Needless to say, Gus, Tony and Monty responded by appearing for dinner immaculately turned out in their best civilian suits, a stipulation requested by their hosts; their kit having all being flown out, including the 'civvies', by their ground crew transport a day or so before they arrived with the B15.

The differences between the American way and the British way were obvious. The Americans were totally war orientated in every-thing they did and all aspects of the American military presence were big. That was fully intentional; they had big bases, large numbers of planes, large quantities of personnel, and enough supplies and support to show it all off to anyone who cared to take a look. Gus, Monty and Tony were rather more used to the quieter, rather understated way the British military did things, but nonetheless they soon got the hang of doing it the American way, especially on the R&R side of the visit.

Back at work, surprisingly fit and well considering how much we had accepted the hospitality of our hosts in Osaka, we all became familiar with another Canberra variant, the US-built version, the Martin B57. Then followed some serious bombing practice and formation flying with our USAF counterparts.

The skip bombing techniques we were shown and had the opportunity to practise were great fun, as we had to perfect this procedure with a bull's-eye type of target just off the coast near Kadena. It might not have seemed such fun if we had known at the time it was a technique they were developing to throw napalm around. I know we were all professional members of Her Majesty's armed forces, but when we talked about it later, none of us were at all comfortable with the idea and were thankful that it was in some ways a theoretical exercise, as napalm was not a standard part of our Squadron's ordnance inventory.

We followed the same route home as we had coming out to Kadena but stopped overnight at Clarke AFB for a bit more of the 'getting to know you,' routine. It was all superbly civilised.

The following month was equally busy, with a great deal more bombing practice and extensive low-level cross-country exercises, including one to Hong Kong, again in 209. Kai Tak was an unusual airport with a very interesting, some would say focusing, curved approach. I cannot recall ever looking up at the nearby buildings with only a few hundred feet to go before touchdown, or at being able to look fairly closely at someone's washing as I descended past it to the runway threshold, but at Kai Tak I could – even through my very restricted vision panel. Fortunately Gus had been taken there before and shown the ropes. Apparently there was a rule in the Kai Tak ops manual that stated any pilot acting as P1 (first pilot), had to have flown in before he was allowed to make an approach himself – very wise!

We stayed overnight near Kai Tak and were amazed to find that the noise and hubbub from the traffic and population only stopped between 2 and 5 am. (We noticed that quite accurately as we only seemed able to get some sleep after 2 am and were woken again at

5 am the same morning when the early risers started the city up again, ready for the next day.) I found it a strange place; it seemed to be the shopping centre for the world, surrounded by widespread and abject poverty. It was a heady mix that I found difficult to take in.

At one stage I remember being offered a young child to buy for just a few pence. (Actually one Hong Kong dollar – or to put it in perspective, one pound was worth sixteen Hong Kong dollars at the time.) 'You can look after him and give him a better life than I can.' I declined both the child and its parents' entreaties. My reaction was one of total sadness, having fairly recently enjoyed the delights of parenthood for the first time. I was not quite ready for that one, and felt quite guilty about our affluent lifestyle compared with the pitiful existence that these people faced.

Back at Tengah it was mostly more low-level navigational exercise consolidation. Tony recorded seven such exercises in total for the month of May – a record. However, there were a few variations with a couple of air tests of both planes and pilots. Early in the month he was assigned to navigate his new Wing Commander, W/Cdr Pedder, on Operation 'Fire Power'. More of the 'Top Brass' followed in June as he and Gus took Air Vice-Marshal Headlam on a tour of several nearby ANZUK bases in a T4, and over the three days of the sortie took him to the bases at Bangkok, Ubon, Abon and Chiang Mai. This was to check their readiness for the perceived ongoing and increasing threat from Communist insurgents in the area. On that trip they again received the very best of treatment and stayed in colonial-style lodges with all the luxury they could provide, although the visiting Canberra crews were very aware that the locally based Hunter crews were still housed under canvas! Gus, Monty and Tony returned to Chiang Mai and Bangkok again the following week. Just one cross-country exercise followed in July and Tony headed off for leave and a break from what had been a pretty sustained and constant workload, even if it had been interspersed with one or two really superb periods of socialising.

All this training and operation in flying the flag was mixed with the occasional real live operations supporting the ANZUK ground troops

*dealing with the Communist insurgents in the north of Malaysia
and in Borneo. We were not that heavily involved but it did occur
from time to time, more as a morale-boosting exercise for the lads on
the ground I suspect. For me in my cramped navigator's quarters it
was all very much the same as the training exercise the day before,
and the one the day before that, except that I knew the bombs in the
bomb bay were live, not dummies. From a practical point of view for
a navigator, it was just like any other exercise. However, the fact
that one of the B15s (not ours), returned to Tengah with at least one
bullet hole in the tail, seemed to indicate that not everyone saw it in
the same benign light.*

July and August were traditional months for summer holidays
and at Tengah this was no exception. The Golds family headed to
the welcoming coolness of the beaches and hills of the local holiday
areas. They took the train out of Singapore to Kuala Lumpur,
where they stayed overnight, then onward the next morning to
Butterworth and the delightful Penang Island, thus discovering
one of the world's holiday hot spots a good two or three decades
before the package tourist industry arrived. They also went to
the Cameron Highlands, where at over 8,000 feet they had to use
blankets for the first time in a very long while, and where they
revelled in the coolness of the air as they explored the delights of
an area of the country that allowed them to walk around in comfort
for hours on end.

The time spent relaxing quickly passed and by late August Tony
was back at work with two air tests of two of the T4s (847 and 841)
with S/Ldr Carruthers. It was S/Ldr Carruthers who was his pilot
for the next two trips on 27 and 29 August. The first was a high-
level cross-country at night and the second a low-level, daytime
cross-country. Then on 30 and 31 August he was off to Labuan
once more, this time with F/Lt Dickie Duke and again with a high-
ranking Army officer as their VIP passenger. Yet again in full
uniform, their VIP suffered mightily from heat and perspiration
problems as they came in to land at Labuan. Obviously, the lessons
had not yet been passed along the line.

*I then met up and flew with my old mentor F/Lt Rickards during the
first week of September. One check ride to start with in a T4, then a*

couple of trips in the B15. Somewhere between the 6th and 9th Gus received his promotion and we celebrated in true RAF style in the Officers' Mess, on his Mess bill – naturally. Mid week saw some more formation practice, first with Gus, then with F/O Pearce on the 13th, who by the time I flew with him two days later on the 25th, had also been promoted to Flight Lieutenant. The drinks were on him that evening after flying; it was starting to look like a pretty good month.

The last two flights at the end of the month were with Gus and Monty. We were let loose with the latest propelled rockets, and allowed to practise our delivery methods. Now our dive techniques were really put to the test. Pull ups of 4 G at something like 300 feet were pretty concentrating, but the negative G forces at the start of the dive sequence were the real killers. We transited at low level and then at the appropriate time, pulled up to 2,000 feet, bunted over and screamed down towards the target at about forty-five degrees. From where I was sitting (if that really is the correct terminology for hanging like a rag doll in your straps) it seemed more like ninety degrees! We started to pull out at about 500 feet and the rockets went on their merry way at about 250 feet to 350 feet.

It was quite noticeable how our voices changed under the strain of pulling so much G. With both dive-bombing techniques it varied. For bomb dropping my voice would be loud and positive, whereas with the rocket firing being at the lower level, it started loud and high pitched and increased in volume and became shriller as the ground approached and the G loads increased. I put that down to a mixture of straining muscles and controlled fear!

I had a set procedure for dealing with the physical problems this brought on. At about 800 feet I would tense all my muscles between waist and thigh, and I do mean all; that helped me deal with it, stay conscious, and generally prevent my stomach divesting itself of my latest meal. It was reckoned that most of the boys could do eight of these manoeuvres before their digestive systems rebelled. I was fortunate and could just reach nine, no more. I expect there was the odd 'bod' who could make ten, but I never came across him. I knew one or two of the other lads whose system went into tilt at six or seven, there was just nothing anyone could do about it. We tried to avoid exploring the limits on that one, as we were all wearing oxygen masks for the duration of the whole manoeuvre. To add to our woes on these sorties, the B15s were also fitted with cameras to record our success, or lack of it, during these particular exercises.

On the lighter side of Tengah life, there was still some good sport to be played. I particularly enjoyed the inter-force golf games where the Squadron played the Army and the aircrews of other squadrons. The prize for the winners of each hole was a pint of iced beer. Our team always made sure that we lost the first six or seven holes. That way, however badly we played, we were guaranteed to win the whole event. A bit sneaky I know, but it paid off every time. I was just surprised that no one ever caught on – or perhaps they did?

Wednesday 2 October saw a new and fortunately short change of address and accommodation for Tony and the rest of the crew of 641. They flew to the jungle airfield of Kuantan, some fifty-five flying minutes' up-country, surrounded by jungle, jungle and yet more jungle. This was operational training for real and for the first time ever for the Ross crew, it was in tented accommodation. The only real permanent construction on the airfield was the ATC centre, although the toilet and shower block was fairly robust and made of wood. Having said all that, the facilities were adequate and the food was good. The cooled beer and a plentiful ration of chilled hygienic water, made the place very bearable for the short period they were there. Tony did six bombing exercises, mainly with Gus, but one each with S/Ldr Carruthers and F/O Butler. All were to their usual ranges at China Rock and Song-Song. The last trips of the month included a further sortie to Labuan, this time with another enjoyable two-day stopover in Hong Kong on the way out. Although he did not know at the time, it would be Tony's last flight ever with Gus and Monty.

My two-year tour was drawing to a close, and along with the other guys who were moving on I was duly summoned to the Squadron CO's office to hear my fate. I was going to tankers. I was also being awarded the GSM Brunei Medal for my efforts over the past two years. The first week of November I did a couple of trips, one with W/Cdr Pierce who was about to be promoted to G/Cpt and would soon take over as Station Commander. Then on the 11th, once the promotion had been announced and the transfer of command had taken place, I flew with him, as the new Station Commander, up to Butterworth for one last time. When 642's wheels touched down at Tengah at 1345 hours that November afternoon it was all over and I was on my way back to England and the Valiant tanker fleet.

Gus and I had our medals presented by the Air Vice-Marshal at the last of the Saturday parades that we would ever attend at Tengah. Full dress uniform was the order of the day with epaulettes, highly polished shoes, and all the formal trimmings of a British military parade very much in evidence.

My log book was just short of 850 hours. With the tanker conversion coming up, the magic 1,000-hour entry could not be so far away.

CHAPTER 4

Gaydon, Marham and Valiants

The sleek Comet Four of RAF Transport Command whisked us home in abject luxury. More so than we had expected because young John took the eye of the Casevac (Casualty Evacuation) nurse on the flight and as she had little to do she almost adopted him for the whole flight. This left Pamela and me to really enjoy the flight and all it had to offer. I recall we had one breakfast on the leg across the Indian Ocean between Tengah and RAF Gan in the Maldives, then another breakfast as we left Gan for RAF Lyneham.

Because of the speed and endurance of the Comet, we were able to keep pace with the time zones and, incredible as it seemed, to land at Lyneham at the same time that we had taken off from Tengah. A common enough occurrence in later years, but at the beginning of the era of jet airliner travel it was quite something, even for us 'hardened' jet crews.

England, when we arrived, seemed bloody cold. Having spent two years in the tropics, Pamela and I really noticed it. Young John, however, had no knowledge of anything else except soaring temperatures and as such had no real experience of having to wear clothes for warmth. He really struggled for a while to understand this new concept in his young life. After the formalities and a stopover at Lyneham, Cleethorpes was our next destination and a fairly short stay including Christmas with Pamela's family. Regrettably the temperature as we headed into January did not seem to improve at all.

45

The Golds family took an apartment near Warwick, close to RAF Gaydon, deep in hunting, shooting and fishing country. They found the lifestyle most agreeable, but somewhat restricted as their interests seemed more diverse than those of their hosts, whose only hobbies seemed to be restricted to hunting, shooting and fishing. A few days after moving in, the ground school training for conversion to the Valiant tanker started. The first three months were virtually all classroom-based and the members of 107 Course at No. 232 OCU, could but glance longingly out of the windows and across the aprons at the huge tankers, as the crews on the course ahead of them headed out on an almost daily basis to practise and perfect their airborne skills in these huge aircraft.

About this time Tony rushed back to Romford to meet up with one of his late father's old bosses, Mr May of May's Motors. May's Motors held the Ford dealership in the area, and some of the savings collected during Tony's posting at Tengah were destined to purchase a new car. A top of the range Ford Zodiac, complete with all the factory extras available, was the chosen vehicle. So thanks to a rather generous deal worked out by Mr May, by the time the course had started, the Golds family had taken delivery of their new car.

As enjoyable as the pride of ownership of the Zodiac was to Tony, it was the ground school that was to fully occupy his mind initially, as he was now in big league navigation. The course was 100 per cent navigation with totally dedicated issues and lectures to attend. It was a hard course and there was a great deal more to get to grips with than on previous occasions. There were state-of-the art navigation systems, including new and more sophisticated compasses to learn and understand; both how they were to use them when airborne and how they were to calibrate them for themselves, when on the ground. The Valiant carried a five-man crew, so there were many new crew operations and procedures to learn. For Tony there was also the all important coordination function with the radar-navigator to learn and understand and to coordinate with his function in the team, particularly during the refuelling phase of the flight. The instructors were always emphasising that in air to air refuelling, the whole aircraft operation was a team effort, and nothing less than full effort from them would be acceptable on the course or when they eventually reached their squadron. On top of all this, there was a heightened awareness amongst them all for the need for pin-point accuracy in everything that they did. It was a bigger aircraft, and a more strategically important role they were undertaking than they had flown before. But above all else was the fact that another RAF aircraft and crew were relying on them to get it right. It all had to be 100 per cent professional, all the time, every time.

Not surprisingly the social life of the OCU and subsequently all its aircrews, was somewhat subdued when compared with their previous RAF life. Yes, certainly Saturday evening was sacrosanct for a good night out, but weekday evenings were now off-limits to partying and heavy Mess evenings. As well as that, some of the crews were still living at RAF Marham, and needless to say, returned home to their families for the weekend. For Tony there was also the obvious fact that the Golds family was now three. Young John was a lively and inquisitive two-and-a-half year old, fascinated by fires, colours and the growing television service now readily available. Pamela took care of the bulk of the parental duties as Tony's spare time was generally filled with revision, course-work and reading up on the subjects associated with the Valiant course.

Pamela was totally supportive during this time and really great at organising things so that I had the time I needed to study. So much so that even during regular visits by friends and family I was able to sneak up to the study and immerse myself in my bookwork, and she would cover for me. My life-long love of playing sport was also put well and truly on the back burner at this time, such was the need to learn the subjects and pass the course.

There were five full aircrews going through 107 Course in March 1964. Each individual was assigned to a specific crew, even if we were not to officially start working together until some five weeks into the course; though not surprisingly we did not fly together as a crew very often. Initially we back-seat boys would be paired up with an experienced pilot and co-pilot and naturally Jeremy and Keith were assigned to work with the more experienced navigators based at Gaydon.

My crew comprised:

S/Ldr Jeremy Price – Pilot
F/Lt Keith Evans – Co-pilot
F/O Tony Golds – Nav/Plotter
F/O Dave Ellis – Nav/Radar
Sgt 'Smithy' Smith – Air Electronics Officer (AEO)

Coupled with the individual skills we had to perfect, there were also the more common aspects of flying the Valiant to learn. How to get in (usually quite a squeeze but a pretty orderly operation) and of course how to get out in an emergency (hopefully just as orderly, but less of a squeeze, as both pilots had Martin-Baker bang-seats to help them on their way). We three back-room boys had our own small escape hatch and a 'gravity operated' method of departure (i.e. we jumped out of the aircraft through the open door). Our rocket assisted colleagues in the front 'office' would have been long gone by the time we had made our exit. It was very focussing to practise the procedure, but fortunately in my entire flying career I never once had to do it for real.

By now the nicknames, except Smithy's, had disappeared and the whole crew relationship became much more professional. The mantra of the course, 'you now get it right every time ... everyone depends on you', became the watchwords of every member of every crew. We were subjected to tests each week, mainly to reassure the instructors that we had absorbed all the information they had thrown at us during the previous few days. We worked for many hours in individual simulators to become fully conversant with the new kit and the new procedures, and it was only on the last day of March that we actually got our hands on a real plane. The Vickers Valiant was a large and impressive aircraft by anyone's standards. Our tankers were a variant of the original Valiant nuclear bomber, and it still appeared the same from the outside as its bomb-carrying brothers.

It looked as if it should be complicated, but it wasn't, and it looked as if it should be spacious inside but it wasn't. Once again, my workstation was very compact and I had no external window, however small, so in some ways the dear old Canberra had been better. My opposite number the Navigator/Radar Operator had the window seat, however the window was minute and the vision very restricted.

Coupled to that, the three of us sat facing the rear of the aircraft, so in reality he could only see a very small area of the ground we had already passed over, and the Nav/Plotter and the AEO could see nothing. Not a lot of use for visual references, but that was one of the pilot and co-pilot's many responsibilities anyway.

The pattern of our working life started with our first training flight. There was a three-hour build up towards any exercise or operation. I allowed at least one hour for my navigation preparation. We then all needed one hour for food, drink, attending the loo and kitting up for the flight, then a further hour to be taken to the plane, climb aboard, settle in and get the aircraft ready for flight. For me this final hour included getting the very latest weather forecasts, both at the home base for take-off and again for landing and for the en-route conditions. Of course I also needed to know of any NOTAM updates that might affect our planned route or any likely alternates, because our routes now frequently had us transiting via civil airways and mixing with the commercial jets carrying out their normal scheduled flights. Fortunately our navigation systems were much superior to those on board a Canberra and well up to the job. We were also fitted with TACAN (Tactical Air Navigation), Marconi Doppler Radar and a variety of additional instruments that all now featured as part of my pre-flight checks.

Tuesday 31 March 1964 was the big day. Tony was allotted to Valiant 826 under the command of F/Lt Foreman, to start the flying section of the course and to begin one of the most intensive periods of flying in his life. Over the next month he would complete twenty individual flights with eight different pilots in eight different aircraft. That would add just over seventy-nine hours to his log book and meant that he would have covered somewhere between 25,000–30,000 miles. With several hours' route plotting and flight planning prior to the flight, it was a monstrous workload in anyone's book. It would also be the start of a lifestyle regime change, as all aspects of his life now became subservient to the four to five hours spent airborne.

My first trip in the Valiant was scheduled for a 1500 hours take-off. For me that meant an arrival at the Crew Room in the Operations

Centre to start my pre-flight preparations by 1130 hours at the latest. I already knew it would be a twelve- to fourteen-hour day and because of this I had already drawn the basic route and a couple of the alternates on my maps the day before, following the instructor's briefing. But now I needed the other up-to-date data to finalise the preparation. I needed the latest weather situation, both the current actual at Gaydon and the forecast for 1900 hours. It was also essential to have the en-route weather conditions as well as the upper wind speeds, plus of course all the NOTAMS likely to affect our route or any likely alternate route we might have to use. There was a pretty full workload, including the interface with the civil aviation centres to enable us to avoid airways and airport infringements.

We then all met up and I gave the crew my briefing. The other crewmembers, led by the pilot, then added their input, including the fact that the flight had been cleared by Ops, that the plane had been released to service by the ground crew and that the transport boys had got a crew-bus organised to take us out to the aircraft. When this was completed there were about two hours to go to departure and we all headed off to the canteen for the pre-flight meal. This was always superb and plentiful, whether it was a breakfast, a midday lunch or an evening meal and was always accompanied with an inexhaustible supply of coffee. After this we then headed for the loos and the changing room. As there were no toilets aboard the Valiant, it was essential to evacuate one's system as much as possible prior to flight, the possible result of not doing so would be dire. Hardly surprisingly, the consequences of forcibly performing this function successfully for years on end, were also pretty damaging on the human system, but the surgeons at the local RAF Hospital in Ely were good and well practised at sorting that particular problem. They were used to seeing a regular flow of tanker and bomber aircrew through their doors for drastic surgical action, once the Marham Medical Centre's creams and ointments became ineffective.

Once the toilet task was completed, we suited up, collected our 'bone-domes', and checked out our personal R/T (radio telegraphy) equipment and our oxygen masks on the test rigs in the room. With about an hour to go, we picked up our kit and trooped out to our waiting bus.

Our Valiant 826 was huge and imposing in its anti-flash, all-white, paint scheme. The top of its main-wheel tyres came dead level with my eyes. OK, I wasn't the tallest chap in the crew, but I still felt that was pretty impressive. We literally threw our nav-bags and flight-bags through the hatch and clambered aboard.

The ground power units that fed electricity to the plane were humming to themselves as we arrived and the lights in the aircraft were already on. It was cramped enough for five crewmembers, but on this first trip I also had an instructor sitting right behind me monitoring my progress, which made it really cosy! I wasn't nervous at all, but I was very conscious of trying to make a good impression. The word round the OCU was that if you did a good job on the first trip, chances were that you never had an instructor fly with you again. That was incentive enough for me, I hadn't gone through all this to have someone looking over my shoulder all the time; besides that, my experience on Canberras taught me independence and I wanted that with the new aircraft and crew as soon as it was permitted.

The AEO went through the checklist with the captain and one by one the engines were started. I was pleased how quiet the cabin was, compared with my dear old Canberra. With all engines running I was then able to switch all my kit on and get started. I had already checked my oxygen and we had all completed the R/T check to ensure we could communicate with each other. The pilot and co-pilot went through their own extensive checklist while we all listened in as our take-off time approached. With about five or six minutes to go, F/Lt Foreman called us each in turn for a final check, the engines increased in noise and we rolled gently forward towards the runway.

The Valiant's four water-injected Rolls-Royce Avon turbojets raised their voices in unison in response to the pilot's push on the throttle levers and I felt the full effect of almost 40,000 pounds of thrust as 826 thundered down Gaydon's two miles of main runway. When we lifted off I recall that although the rearward-facing seating position seemed obviously different than that of my first love, the dear old Canberra, it was by no means uncomfortable. At 1,000 feet I switched my instruments on to full power, having remembered my instructor's dire warnings of the effect that full power would

*have on the instruments while on the ground. I re-checked my
oxygen supply, logged the take-off time and updated my flight plan
accordingly. I was determined to get it right first time and put up a
good show. I was the only Flying Officer amongst the Nav/Plotters,
and the only ex-Canberra chap on the course. I felt I had a point
to prove. Despite the workload on my first 'real' flight, I found it
totally exhilarating.*

Thus began the intensive airborne side of the conversion training
for the new boys of 107 Course. It would continue unabated for
them for the next thirty-five days as they put into practice all they
had learned in the previous weeks of ground school. Initially there
was a series of four exercises in four days, with those on 1, 2 and
3 April all having a ten o'clock or 1030 hours take-off time. That
meant very early morning starts for them all. Then it eased off
slightly and exercises came up more or less every other day,
but then towards the end of the month, coinciding with the start
of night exercises, the four flights in four days routine kicked
in again. There was no let up, and no passengers carried on this
course. Tony's section of the rearward-facing desk became part
of a familiar routine to him and he soon started to feel as much
at home there as he had in the Canberra. He flew with a different
pilot on each occasion in the last week, then on the first Monday
in May, he completed his final four and a half-hour exercise
with W/Cdr Steele and his OCU training at Gaydon was over.
Marham, Norfolk and Squadron life was beckoning.
    In-flight refuelling was still a bit of a novelty at that time, so
there was a lot of emphasis on setting or breaking records and
milking as much publicity for it (and the RAF), as possible. One
record the new boys did not need was to be late for work. They
were in essence undergoing continuation training on the Squadron;
but now Squadron rules applied. Work started promptly at 0915
hours. If anyone arrived at 0916 hours they attracted for themselves some extra duties; not a desired scenario for new boys still
learning the job. Despite the thoroughness of the course at Gaydon
there was still a lot to learn in order to become proficient at the
new role. It was a step up into the big league; it was time to get
stuck in.

At that time there were no married quarters available at Marham as it was awash with young Flight Lieutenants with two children. Being a Flying Officer with one child I did not even reach the bottom of the last page of the allocation list, so Pamela and I opted to buy our own place. By chance we came across a small development in West Winch, to the south of King's Lynn, where one of the previous deals had fallen through. It suited us perfectly; we had the deposit and were not part of a chain, and were therefore available to move in the day it was ready – the developer welcomed us with open arms. It was all we could hope for; it had double glazing, central heating, a good-size garden space and was located in an area where there was a strong social life, which kicked into place as soon as we moved in. With my home life settled and my promotion to Flight Lieutenant confirmed in mid-January, it was now a matter of really getting fully up to speed with the job. There was not even a Mess shindig to celebrate my promotion. It had been expected and was considered the norm.

During the first few flights I was rapidly made aware we were not the only planes in the sky. With the Canberra we were able to operate at a height where we were exclusive owners of the airspace we flew in. Now some 20,000 feet lower, we had to learn to share the sky with other aircraft, both military and civilian. It was a whole new concept! As well as this we had to learn to cover long distances using the designated airways under civilian control. For me that meant continually checking updates on NOTAMs, procedures, airfield operating regulations and frequencies in use. Above all, I had to make sure I always had the most up-to-date data with me in my flight bags. I use bags plural, because from my first flight in the Valiant until my last in the Victor, like all Nav/Plotters, I always needed two to carry all the vast quantity of paperwork and charts required.

Just to keep us on our toes, these bags were occasionally spot checked. Woe betide any aircrew who had an out-of-date piece of data lurking in either bag. We had to hand in all our paperwork and the marked-up maps at the end of each sortie, after the de-brief, so they could be securely stored for six months in case there were any complaints, infringements or incidents to sort out. Fortunately this was an extremely rare occurrence.

This enormous quantity of paperwork cannot be understated. There were all the NOTAMS, the Royal Flight (Purple Airways) listings, the log keeping for the flight itself and the current data required for any chosen route. All this had to be prepared before the briefing, prior to take-off, as well as both the alternative routes chosen and the data on the airfields designated as alternative landing destinations. Nav/Plotters had to log the aircraft position five minutes after take-off, and thereafter every fifteen minutes as well as five minutes after a designated turning point and again every fifteen minutes after the turning point. They were all kept very busy throughout the flight. Although the fuel availability was the province of the flight crew, it was also the Nav/Plotter who kept them updated with positional reports and distance to cover, to aid them with their fuel calculations.

Ironically, Tony's first duty on the Squadron was a QFI's (Qualified Flying Instructor) check flight for the pilot, at Gaydon. So for his first real sortie he headed back south to his old training base, then after lunch, flew the two-hour sortie needed for F/Lt Edwards to be cleared by the QFI. It was then a quick hop back to Marham, logging three hours and thirty-one minutes for the whole trip. That was also the total time for the day and as it was their only flight in May, for the month.

It was now heading into summer, so it was high time for Tony to take a spot of leave, relax and start to enjoy his new home. Although the house and most of the furniture, fixtures and fittings were all sparkling new, there was still a great deal of work needed on the garden, and he had just a couple of weeks to get started. Somehow Garden Leave only seemed to arrive at the RAF's convenience, not his!

By July we were working for real. In at the deep end so to speak, as we were allocated two aircraft to refuel. The first was another Valiant and the second was a Lightning, one of the UK's front-line fighters. That trip was a full four hours and twenty-five minutes' airborne. A second Lightning was our receiver a week later, and we all started to settle back into Squadron life again. August was really busy and our 'customers' included another Lightning, a Vulcan and a Victor, both the latter being part of our nuclear deterrent V-bomber force.

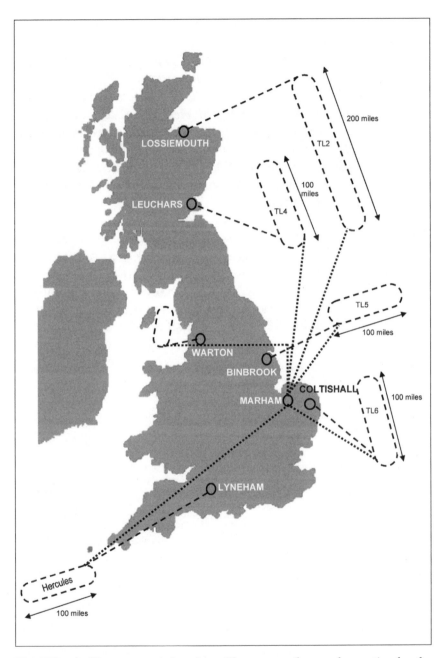

The UK refuelling racetrack locations. These were the regular sorties for the Marham Tanker fleet.

The other highlight was reaching my 1,000 hours. The actual 1,000-hour point occurred about halfway through a training exercise on Wednesday 19 August in Valiant 390, flown by F/Lt Peach. It had taken me just over four years to get there.

The weather was great, so a late summer break seemed logical and some further work on the garden in West Winch was called for. When I returned from leave it seemed a little quiet and there were just a couple of trips in September to complete. One a five-hour night navigation exercise with F/Lt Strachan then three days later on the 10th, a Javelin refuelling operation, which we completed in just over three and a half hours.

November was all about a short detachment to Cyprus. The Valiant crews were repositioned out in a C130 to operate from Akrotiri, in support of the Lightnings stationed there. However, when Tony arrived there were already several crews available and subsequently the workload was light. He was therefore able to enjoy the many facilities that Akrotiri had to offer, both on and off

The standard racetrack pattern for the tankers when operating out of Cyprus. Refuelling was always over the sea, and wherever possible over international waters.

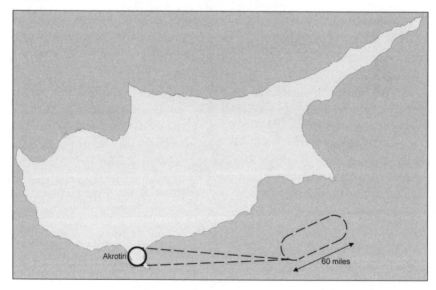

the base. The late autumn sun in the Eastern Mediterranean was a very welcome diversion.

By now the wing spar problem on the Valiant was becoming a major concern. We had all heard of of the problem of the plane diverted into Manston, and the Engineering Section was abuzz with the rumour that the fatigue cracking affected the greater majority of the Valiant fleet. Although several planes were cleared to continue to fly, it became increasingly obvious that big decisions were being made in the MoD and that the situation might soon change. Tony did three refuelling flights in November: a Javelin on Bonfire Night, a Lightning on the 12th and another Javelin on the 19th. When he stepped out of 812 just before 2.30 that Thursday afternoon, he little realised that he would never set foot aboard a Valiant again.

We found out about the tanker's demise at one of our regular daily briefings. At 9.15 we officially knew nothing, by 9.30 we knew it was all over. It was that quick. Certainly the rumours had been flying thick and fast, but this was the official confirmation. With the security of the job and the pay, I initially thought it would be good and that my further allocation of Garden Leave would really get my garden sorted. But the reality when we thought about it was far more serious, particularly for some of the senior boys. Those heading towards the end of their flying tours might never fly again, and our well knit ground support teams were sure to be broken up. Many of the chaps who were in married quarters were staring ahead at months of leave, with little or nothing to do. For them it was catastrophic. As the days passed many simply turned up for duty every day regardless, to drink coffee, chat, or sit around in the Mess. Their lives were on hold until the system got them re-assigned or posted. My garden in West Winch flourished.

CHAPTER 5

Marham and Victors

Just one year after starting ground school at 232 OCU for the Valiant, I was back at 232 OCU Marham starting the similar course for the Victor. I had not been totally idle during my extended Garden Leave. I had managed to get three flights back in the dear old Canberra at Bassingbourn, where a re-write of the checklist was being undertaken. I was delighted to return to the air in anything that flew, and very pleased to be doing something other than domestic horticulture. However, along with most of the rest of the team at 214 Squadron, I really thought the re-write was a bit of a waste of time, as in the mid-1960s, the 1940s design of the Canberra was surely getting close to the end of its service life. Like so many other 'experts' in the field of aviation, I could not have been more wrong. In reality, the RAF career of the Canberra had not even reached the halfway mark – it still had several decades of useful, active life before its decommissioning in 2006.

Back at 232 OCU Marham, it was more of the same, this time with the Handley-Page Victor Mk 1 tanker in mind. The powers that be in the MoD or the Treasury or both for all I knew, had decreed that the costs of the repair programme to the Valiant fleet were totally unjustifiable and therefore the UK's airborne refuelling commitment would fall to the Victors of 214 Squadron at RAF Honington.

So it was that after a few weeks of ground school on Tuesday 4 May I was again being driven out of the Operations Centre to a new aircraft type and the first day of a full and hectic month of airborne training and familiarisation exercises.

The Victor was a beautiful-looking aircraft and I was looking forward to getting to grips with it, and to meeting up again with Jeremy Price, whom I knew had also moved across to train on the Victor.

May was all training of one sort or another, including a short Marham-to-Gaydon sortie on the 25th, with F/Lt Galliene. I flew with Jeremy four times that month, and really started what was to be a very long crew association with him. By the end of the course I had nearly forty-five hours on Victors, almost half the total hours I had amassed on the Valiant in nine months.

The Victor was similar in size to the Valiant, although it had less power available and therefore had a lower rate of climb. On the plus side, the crew space was a tiny bit more generous and there were not so many sextant readings needed, thanks to the latest navigation kit that was fitted, so from that point of view it was quite an improvement. However, there was still no vision panel and we three rear cockpit crewmembers had no ejection seats at our disposal. We still faced rearwards, and from my point of view it still necessitated the continuous mental juggling of re-orientating everything in my head 180 degrees, when relating it to the aircraft and the true direction of travel.

In reality the training on the Victor course was shorter and nowhere near as demanding as the earlier Valiant course. It would be fair to say it was more of a top-up situation than a full blown aircraft conversion. The Nav/Radar man had one of the biggest changes; this time instead of a single refuelling drogue, there were three, although in fact it was standard practice only to use the outer two wing drogues. The three trailing drogues configuration that really looked most impressive was in reality more of an air-display only scenario. There was also a camera available for the Nav/Radar operator to actually see all that was going on. This was a great improvement.

Training progressed well during the month of May, and after twenty-eight and a quarter hours' daylight flying and sixteen hours and ten minutes' night flying, they were ready for Squadron duties. However, once again the RAF had a neat twist in the tail to add to the proceedings. 214 Squadron and RAF Honington were not to be and the newly qualified crews headed to 55 Squadron, just across the apron at Marham. For Tony this was very much a good move. John was happily settled at school in King's Lynn and, for once, their delay in deciding whether or not to put their house on the market worked in their favour as it meant they would stay in West Winch and avoid the upheaval of moving. On the down side, Tony had already spent quite some time helping to set up the now redundant Operations and Planning room at RAF Honington with his old chum Sam Ryder. He had enjoyed working with Sam, and in reality binning several maps that he had carefully marked-up was no big deal; after all, that was effectively what happened after every tanker flight anyway as far as he was concerned. He rarely if ever referred to his maps again after use, having handed them in at the post-flight briefing after each sortie.

21 and 23 June '65 were really check-out flights for the new pilot, and of course a high element of showing off the Victor tanker to every-one. Then on Wednesday the 30th it was a five-hour, forty-five minute marathon shake-down of the whole plane and all its systems for the whole crew. Due to the fact that it was a new plane to us, it was a long hard process for everyone, especially Jeremy. The Victor Mk 1 had a braking chute rather than the assistance of the big 'barn-door' sized flaps that he was used to on the Valiant and due to its small wheels it also had a minimal reserve in its braking system. Certainly, if the chute failed to deploy on landing, it was almost a forgone conclusion that you would burn the brakes out stopping the plane sufficiently to keep it on the runway. After that first real 'full on' sortie, every one of us in the crew slept soundly that night when we got home – we were all totally bushed.

July was devoted to practising with the new aircraft, and becoming familiar with its systems and our role in using them. Our 'A' Flight Nav-Leader was my old friend, and Nav-Leader from Tengah, Senior F/Lt Wotherspoon. He was a great help as we worked up to becoming fully operational. However, all our good work was beginning to pay off and we soon started to do the job for real. After a three and a half-hour sortie with F/Lt Russell that was part daylight and part night, I was crewed up again with Jeremy and I

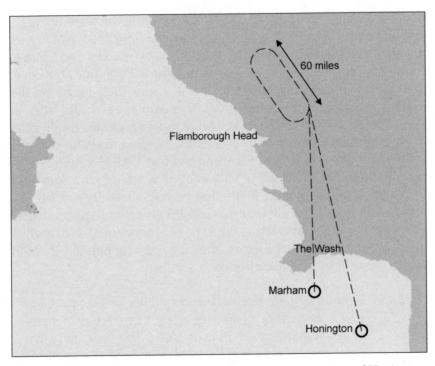

The standard racetrack pattern for the tankers when operating out of Honington. Refuelling was always over the sea, and wherever possible over international waters.

started tanking duties for real, with a pair of Lightnings on the 24th and 25th.

September was a busier month with several more Lightning refuelling trips. It was, however, the sortie on the first of the month that was the most unusual, as we at RAF Marham, played host to a BBC film crew. (All part of showing off the UK's new air to air refuelling capability to the whole world.) We were the reserve crew and as such flew the practice sortie along with the primary crew chosen for the role. We consoled ourselves that it was the planes and the refuelling kit they were interested in, and we were not too put out missing any of the 'Lights, Camera, Action,' stuff.

October and November saw a number of similar refuelling sorties and a two-day trip to Luqa as part of the build-up to taking a squadron of Lightnings down there on detachment. By late November we were starting to use the racetrack pattern with the receiver aircraft. This was new for us and also new for some of the Lightning pilots; unsurprisingly these flights were sometimes rather long, drawn out affairs as the pilots adjusted to their new airborne refuelling procedures.

The Victor tankers had two red lines painted under each wing. These were used by the receiver planes as guide markers for their pilots to align their planes, so that the receiver pod on the tanker and the pick-up probe on their plane connected. The Lightning pilots needed this set-up as they could not see the receiver probe on their planes, which were effectively located behind their right

The standard racetrack pattern for the tankers when operating out of Malta. Refuelling was always over the sea, and wherever possible over international waters.

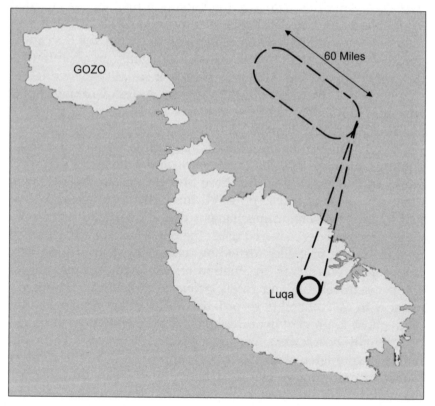

ear and therefore totally out of sight. The repeated practice enabled them to position their aircraft with their chosen line to achieve a positive hook-up. Experienced fighter pilots often had a chosen rivet on the underside of the wing of the tanker that they used for visual reference instead of the red lines, and using this refinement to the standard procedure, could 'hit' the mark every time. At the other end of the scale it was not unknown for the new pilots not to achieve hook-up at all during a practice sortie and eventually be called off to return to base before their fuel ran out. It was a learning curve they all had to master before they could be sent overseas.

The wing drogue part of the Victor refuelling system was a remarkably successful unit considering it was a bit of a last-minute conversion from the standard one used by the Buccaneer. They supplemented the Hose Drum Unit (HDU) known to all as 'Hoodoo'. After the demise of the Valiant, something was needed in double-quick time, and this was it. Remarkably, all that was required was a mid-system holding tank to change the Buccaneer 'buddy-buddy' system from a one-shot capability, to a continuous flow refuelling system. That may well over simplify the work that was needed in that short time to get the system working, but it was most certainly one of the most successful quick-fix pieces of engineering in RAF history.

The fuel came from the Victor's main feeder tank to the small holding tank in the refuelling pods slung under the Victor's crescent wing, and thence out to the hose and drogue to the receiving plane. The hose unit was powered through a small gearbox that had a simple reversing mechanism that allowed the hose to be either deployed or recovered using the power generated by a small forward-facing propeller turned by the airflow. It was not a very fast system, but it was, in aviation terms, totally simple, almost 100 per cent reliable and rarely prone to any sort of failure. To assist with this reliability record, there was a braking mechanism on the hose to prevent over deployment and separation, although occasionally hoses were lost for a variety of reasons. The main failure encountered with the system appeared to be the receiver plane dropping away before it had pulled clear, thus leaving the tanker with the broken-off refuelling probe locked into the drogue. This was a tad embarrassing for the pilot of the receiver plane and an error that was difficult to hide. Certainly, it was one that he could be sure that his fellow pilots and the tanker crews would tease him about for several weeks after it had occurred. (Plinth-mounted refuelling probe ends were not an uncommon presentation item in the Mess!)

With the onset of winter our workload seemed to become busier, with twenty-eight hours to enter in my log book in November and thirty-eight for December. Virtually all were refuelling sorties for the Lightning boys. By now we were not only practising with them, but were also supporting them during their exercises. Although highly satisfying, it was tremendously hard work. On 14, 15 and 16 December I was airborne for a total of twelve hours, working all the time. If you add to that the preparation and de-brief time, that was getting close to a ten- or twelve-hour day for that mid-week series of flights. On 20 December we were grounded by bad weather, and had a very pleasant, if somewhat unexpected, overnight stop at our diversionary airfield, Leconfield. The return home the next day after a very leisurely start was my last flight before Christmas. Three days after Boxing Day we would be back on duty as we were now definitely a fully integrated part of the UK's air to air refuelling capability. It felt really satisfying to be back as part of that team.

Now it was Christmas, and more particularly it was John's first Christmas in England. Being the first grandson on either side of the family, he was badly spoilt, with toys coming at him from all directions. We bought John his own TV set for his bedroom, along with the regulation Action Man toys and a number of Dinky cars and trucks. There was the usual selection of books that Pamela and I used to read to him for the last fifteen or twenty minutes before 'lights out' of an evening. Then last but not least there was Rexy. We thought an animal in the house would assist John's develop-ment, with the learning of responsibility towards the fox terrier that we told him was his. Truth to tell, no one owned Rexy; Rexy owed no allegiance to anyone. Rexy belonged to Rexy. He was one of those dogs who appeared to go through life according to his own rules. He was a real character, almost a total pussy cat indoors that turned into a rabid Rottweiler the moment he stepped outside the door. He loved playing football with John and me (or anyone else who cared to join in for that matter), but had no concept of playing gently and would frequently sink his teeth into the plastic ball with the inevitable result. It became so frequent we actually kept a couple of spare footballs in a cupboard for just such occasions.

Soon after Christmas, certainly before I went back to work, it snowed. The garden became a typical Christmas card scene and we were able to introduce John to the fun side of an English winter with snowmen, snowballs and sledges. Life was just brilliant. We were financially very comfortable and we were fortunate to have great neighbours and friends. Also, the house party scene had re-started for us and we had found a really superb local baby-sitter for the occasions when Pamela and I felt like going out for the evening.

The Christmas period at Marham was also becoming more family orientated as families visited each other over the course of the holiday. However, it was with the New Year's Party that 55 Squadron really excelled itself and a full-scale, old-fashioned, fancy dress party ensued. It started at the Squadron Commander's house and eventually settled in for the night at the Officers' Mess. The Mess staff were brilliant and met us at the door with champagne and ensured we were kept well supplied with both food and drink, all evening. I think the social side of Marham life at that time worked so well because we were in the main, the core of the ex-Valiant team, and were all young and enthusiastic party people, yet still able to be fully professional while doing our job.

This extended across the board in all directions, to the crews' wives, the Support Squadrons, Engineering and all the other sections within RAF Marham who worked with us. We could all socialise well, and over this Christmas, as the Squadron was still in the build-up phase of air to air refuelling and were not on call over the holiday, we made the most of it. As such we were all able to enjoy the break to the full and return to duty totally refreshed and relaxed.

As the saying goes, all good things must come to an end, and for Tony, after a couple of Lightning refuelling jobs on 29 and 30 December, 1966 started off with a full month of flying with either the Squadron Commander or his deputy. That was just over seventeen hours logged with either a Squadron Leader or a Wing

Commander as his pilot. That sort of pattern didn't happen very often. February included a greater percentage of night flights and yet again the task of ferrying Lightnings down to Malta was starting to feature as a regular monthly sortie. March saw the old team back together with Jeremy Price and a variety of tankers either practising or refuelling the Lightnings for real. There were three visits to the nearby station at Wattisham, including a planned low-level fly-past on the morning of 25 March. April was also quiet with just two sorties and two weeks' leave, but May was back with a vengeance with ten sorties and forty-two and a half hours flown, including nearly twelve hours on the Western Ranger exercise. By the time June was over, Tony's first log book was full and a new Form 1767 (Royal Air Force Flying Log Book) was requisitioned. He would need several more of these before he hung up his flight bag for good. The old Form 1767 had 1,422 hours logged in it, in a little over six years. To no one's surprise, the new log started with a rush, recording twelve sorties in the first month. The thirty-five hours logged for July were all flown with the old team, and included a week devoted to ferrying two Lightnings to the Middle East for the Royal Saudi Air Force.

We went out early on the 12th to Cyprus, after a quick stop at Luqa to refuel and to await the arrival of the Saudi's new planes. They landed at Akrotiri, after their own refuelling stop at Malta on the 14th and we took them onward to Riyadh the following day. That was an interesting trip and one that I will never forget. It was the first time we had ever been under any sort of external threat and the first time I had seen the fighters that we were escorting reverse their roles and become our guardians. It was most impressive.

We had planned to go via Syrian airspace into Riyadh. The flight plan had been completed, submitted and accepted in advance by the Syrian Air Traffic Authorities without a hitch, or any hint of what was to follow. So far so good.

We took off from Akrotiri on schedule and climbed in loose formation to our cruise height. We called up Syrian ATC and announced our arrival in their airspace on time, at our planned height and travelling at the speed and direction submitted in the flight plan. The call back from Syrian ATC was not at all what we expected.

'RAF-AIR you are cleared to continue. Escort planes to return to original base.'

Now that was not in the plan at all. Jeremy pressed his PTT (the transmit button on his control column).

'RAF-AIR. Close Formation.'

'RAF-AIR. Close Formation.' The Lightnings acknowledged.

They closed up and came in tight. All the practice flights we had undertaken together were now paying off. Jeremy pressed the PTT again.

'RAF-AIR. Missiles Armed.'

'RAF-AIR. Missiles Armed.' Again the Lightnings acknowledged.

Syrian ATC went quiet, and we carried on along our approved route and into Saudi airspace. At the pre-arranged spot over the vast Saudi desert we gave the fighters their last top-up of fuel, said our goodbyes and turned back to Cyprus. An hour or so later the Saudi ATC handed us back to the Syrian controllers. They made no mention of the earlier incident; nor did we. We then had a very gentle amble back to Marham, staying one more night in Akrotiri and another at Luqa on the way home.

August was a good mix of refuelling trips, exercises, a ferry flight and a display flight. We were still showing off our new toy! In September I went on leave for most of the month and took the family and our young niece Julie (my godchild), for a late summer break to Lloret Del Mar in Catalunya. Later in that month I also entered the shortest time airborne for any month of my entire flying career.

Jeremy and I did a very short ferry flight from Honington to Marham. I logged a whole twenty minutes for the flight, which was also the total for the day and as it happened for the entire month.

As autumn became winter and 1966 drew to a close, more training and more refuelling exercises became the routine. On 5 December, midway through a Towline exercise, in Victor 620, Tony passed the 1,500-hour entry in his log. By the time Jeremy put the plane down on Marham's runway at the end of the sortie, Tony's RAF career had been airborne for 1,503 hours.

Soon a second Christmas at Marham and West Winch was the top priority for the Golds family. Again, RAF Marham, the Officers' Mess, neighbours and family all featured heavily in Tony's

Christmas plans. The spring of 1967 saw the pattern of work continue and life at 55 Squadron proceeded pretty much to plan. Spring followed in much the same way until mid May when Tony learned he was heading back out to the Indian Ocean close to his old base at Tengah. On a short two-week detachment they would be heading to the island airfields of Masirah and Gan, and then on to Butterworth, passing through Akrotiri both on the way out and on the way back. Again, he was teamed up with Jeremy and the usual crew. Victor 589, a plane they had only flown once before, was their allotted aircraft.

That trip was more a paid holiday than work. I'm not sure what Jeremy's official brief was, but it might well have been along the lines ... 'well sod off and have a great time, do enjoy yourselves, and by the way, could you take these two Lightnings with you and refuel them from time to time, that way you at least appear to earn your keep.' Certainly, that was how it panned out. It seemed that the RAF, in its infinite wisdom, gave us our own private jet to play with for a few days, and we took full advantage of it.

We landed in Cyprus, in the late afternoon sunshine. A quick sort of paperwork, and an even quicker shower followed before we headed to the Mess bar. Pimms, whisky and brandy sour were the first rounds. Someone ordered a taxi to go down town for a meal, so there was enough time for another round to be ordered while we were waiting; it was one of those sorts of nights. I recall the kokkinelli was free with the food at the restaurant of choice, and we finished off with Contreau and Turkish Delight. Amazingly we were all fit (well, fit enough) to fly the second leg the following day.

That leg was from Akrotiri to Masirah, a delightful island off the coast of Oman in the Indian Ocean, predominantly high mountains surrounded by vast sandy beaches.

I recall that gin and tonics were the 'in' drink in the Masirah Mess, so who were we to buck the trend? We also managed a game of golf while we were there, even though we were somewhat surprised to find that the greens were sand, sprayed with oil. Common enough in today's world, but still a bit of a novelty in those days.

We were advised to make sure we were not playing after 6.45, as the loss of daylight at that latitude occurred in a few minutes; very costly in the golf ball department. Once dark, there was nothing for it but to head to the swimming pool and the outside bar. The sea always looked inviting for an early evening dip, but there were just too many sting rays, jelly fish and other such 'nasties' in the coastal waters to risk it.

Gan was the next port of call, and was even nicer than Masirah, mainly because there were no mosquitoes on the island at all. It was a delightful place with long stretches of pure white sand surrounded by clear turquoise water that was dotted with local dug-out boats, skimming along under the power of the large outboard motors that hung over their sterns. Lazing on the beach was heaven, but we had to watch the strength of the sun. Severe sunburn was a court marshal offence, and one that would have been far too easy to be lured into. So we tried snorkelling along the inshore to see for ourselves the variety and wonder of the local marine life. This had to be Gan's piéce de resistance.

From there we headed to Butterworth and Penang. Penang was definitely worth the visit. The weather, as at Butterworth, was not too bad, once you got used to the daily downpour! We then refuelled the pair of Lightnings, which were on their way to Tengah, and to our delight were subsequently advised we had done all that was needed, and we could pop off home now. So we did, retracing our route out and including more games of golf and more horse riding at Akrotiri, getting home just in time to take a week's leave. Not a bad life when you think about it – their lordships had really got it right this time!

They spent the following two or three weeks back in the normal 55 Squadron routine of refuelling sorties from Marham, then towards the end of July headed out to the sunny climate of Cyprus again. This time they were refuelling from Akrotiri, usually in an area to the south-east of the island, over the sparkling blue waters of the Mediterranean Sea. It was during these stays in Cyprus that Tony extended his sporting interests and developed a liking for horse riding and as such was able to enjoy some time with the members of the riding clubs around the base. After a couple of weeks' leave in July, the August and September routines were now back firmly in place, although with the end of the two-year tour at 55 Squadron coming up, it was starting to get into the speculation time of 'where to next'. Jeremy Price was unquestionably a superb pilot and destined for higher things within the RAF. To Tony and the rest of his crew, Jeremy was an obvious and worthy officer and deserving of moving up in the RAF hierarchy. Their last flight together was on 15 August for four and a half hours. They would next meet up again as aircrew some six years later on 13 July 1972. The tanker XA937 would be a K1 variant. Unsurprisingly, they would again be refuelling a Lightning.

Towards the end of my tour with 55 Squadron, I was called into the squadron office and informed that my next posting would be at the Joint Air Reconnaissance Intelligence Centre (JARIC) at Brampton, on the outskirts of Huntingdon. Pamela and I talked it through when I arrived home that evening. It would be a major life change. I would no longer be flying for a living and for the first time in my RAF career I would essentially be working at a nine-to-five job. That was certainly different! As part of the plan, we decided that we would sell the house in West Winch and move closer to Huntingdon. It also seemed a sensible move to trade in the Zodiac and purchase two smaller cars.

Things really were changing.

CHAPTER 6

JARIC and a Nine-to-five Job

W hen Tony closed his log book and put it away in the desk drawer at home it had 1,866 hours recorded between its blue covers. It had been a fairly rapid climb to achieve this number, but now it would have to go on hold for a while as he attempted to get to grips with a genuine nine-to-five office job, RAF Brampton's ultra high security regime and a lifestyle that did not involve actually stepping into an aeroplane. It was all rather new and a bit of a novelty. It felt really strange that he could not talk to anyone about his work, even to the chap in the next office. As aircrew, there was always a need to talk about the job, the flight or what they were doing ... it was total teamwork. Now it was a complete contrast – it was almost total isolation. It was also completely alien to him that he could take nothing into the office in the morning or take anything home with him in the evening. If he was in the middle of a job that he really wanted to finish ... and even if he was happy to do it in his own time, it was just not allowed. For his position at JARIC this was simply not on however alien it seemed to him, especially as he was very used to starting before six in the morning one day and finishing after midnight the next. JARIC was nothing like this and being an office-bound person for the first time in his life was going to take quite some adapting to.

Pamela and I had already decided it would make sense to sell the house at West Winch and move nearer Huntingdon. The estate agent came out from King's Lynn and on his first visit we were given the very good news that we would make a really decent profit on our short stay in Long Lane.

A new-build house in the village of Houghton and Wyton was available and it seemed to suit us perfectly. It was on the west side of Huntingdon in the Ouse valley, close to RAF Wyton. In reality it would not be ready for several months, so I settled down to a routine of six o'clock starts in my trusty mini van. However, we were approaching mid-winter, so frost, fog and snow were becoming a regular feature of my dark, early morning drives. Once or twice, when the Gods of the Weather really gave the Ouse valley a hard time, I chickened out and booked into the Officers' Mess for a few days. My situation was not helped with the length of time that the clearance process took to give me the all-clear. I realised it was the same for everyone and I had been pre-warned of the time delay, but it was still pretty frustrating to turn up for work and then not be allowed to do anything. Fortunately there was the standard JARIC induction course to complete, and for me a slight reprieve as the CO gave me a project to keep me from going quietly insane through boredom.

I was asked to produce a block diagram of the departments and their functions within JARIC, taken from the various station administration documents. It was a welcome time filler and it also helped me understand a little about the organisation I was about to join.

Then, of course, there was always sport. I soon made contact with the station hockey club and managed to secure its running as my second duty. Now at least I was back with some like-minded sportsmen. We had three teams – the first and second teams and a six-a-side team for the ex-aircrew chaps. I played with the first team and also trained and travelled with both of the other squads. Our Sergeant PTI (Physical Training Instructor) on the station was also in charge of the aircrew's six-a-side team and that helped enormously with the training programme and arranging the availability of station facilities. I was able to sort the transport for away games, so that side of life was at least getting properly organised. The CO was very amenable and became even more supportive when we started winning *on a regular basis and were able to provide a steady stream of cups, salvers and plaques for the showcase in his office.*

If I was comfortable with my sporting life, then my working life was certainly taking a while to come to terms with. Security at JARIC was high, to the point of being in the stratosphere. You simply could not get onto the unit without the correct credentials; even then, with all the security clearance available, you could only enter your own workplace area. Even the car parks were located outside the high main security fence and there was an abundance of barbed wire that littered the area like Christmas streamers.

In reality, it was the adopted working practice to only go to your own room, as it made things so much simpler. During working hours all rooms were locked from the inside and entry entailed knocking and asking for permission. There was then anything from a two- to ten-minute wait as all desks were cleared of work before admission was permitted. You only made casual visits for a chat once or twice before you realised what a time-consuming performance it was for all concerned to achieve the security level required. Even if the calls were semi-work related, they were soon abandoned when you realised what a pain in the lower parts of the anatomy your visit was to the rest of the chaps in the office being visited.

About six weeks into the year Tony was called into the boss's office and given the all clear to go and start work. His clearance had, unsurprisingly, proved totally satisfactory.

Fortunately for him clearance came after only the standard eight to ten weeks' wait. He later heard of others less fortunate having to wait in excess of twelve weeks to get started. Needless to say, he was working on the navigational side of the operation and generally keeping the maps up to date for the V-bomber force. There were only two Navigational Officers doing this particular task, although they were supported by a superb team of Sergeant and Corporal draughtsmen and cartographers. It was, however, a non-ending job; once one piece of updated intelligence had been added to the maps, then the next piece arrived. This meant it needed inclusion, often with the requirement to revise one of the pre-planned routes that had been carefully worked out earlier, based on previous intelligence reports; it never stood still. Work would start about 8.30 am, certainly not before, as everywhere was under strict security and all documents remained locked up. Then at the end of the day, about 4.30 pm, everyone had to start clearing away so that nothing was left on desks and tables. All documents had to be stored safely away under lock and key, or in some cases, several locks and keys, before the personnel left for the night. There was nothing Tony could do to improve the rigidity and constraints of his professional side of his life; however, there was plenty he could do to make his free time work well for him.

Our new home at Houghton was near the river and close to many fabulous country walks around the Hemingford Grey and St Ives area. It was an idyllic part of the traditional English countryside and we enjoyed it to the full. John settled down well in his new school and having taken to swimming enthusiastically from his early days at Tengah, was delighted when his school chose him to represent them in the Fifty Metre Butterfly race at a local gala. His enthusiasm suddenly dropped off rapidly when he discovered the temperature (or lack of it) of the water in outdoor pools in rural England. At that point all his swimming activities were planted firmly on the back burner.

Our social life was back to full throttle as we had great neighbours again with a selection of very pleasant country pubs within a very short distance from home, and the holiday boating area around the nearby town of St Ives. Many of our closest friends were of course RAF families and wives' groups and coffee mornings for the girls were again becoming the norm for Pamela. Subsequently, baby-sitting and other similar potentially problematical areas of family life were never of any significance within our circle of friends.

Having a nine-to-five job and a very stable and regulated social life did mean I had the time to go back to school, well Cambridge College of Arts and Technology actually, to get an HNC in Business Studies. Pamela and I had been discussing the possibilities of life after the RAF and my need for some more formal qualifications. Business Studies appeared to fit the bill as it seemed to involve some subjects that were new and interesting to me. I really enjoyed the course and found the whole learning process really quite refreshing. I also had a good relationship with most of my lecturers, particularly the ex-Naval Commander from the Royal Naval Legal Department who was the lecturer on the Commercial Law course.

The job at JARIC had not been that exciting, certainly it was nothing when compared with flying on a regular basis, but the surrounding home, sports and social life accompanying it had been really first class and enjoyable ... but where to go next? There were several options offered to me towards the end of my stay at Brampton, all of them quite appealing in their own way. After a quick sort through the list, the posting that really interested me the most, and more importantly had Pamela's seal of approval, was a return to Singapore and RAF Tengah.

CHAPTER 7

Return to Tengah

I n November 1970, the Golds family was once again aboard a
Comet of RAF Transport Command, this time heading back
to Singapore and RAF Tengah. On this occasion it was to be a
one-year posting and a desk job helping the Singapore Air Force
(SAF) in the transfer of the Operations Section at Tengah to their
control and responsibility. Tony's task was to train four SAF
officers assigned to him to be as fully conversant with the most
up-to-date operational practices of the RAF as time permitted, and
to be able to run their own show when he left. They were a bright
and enthusiastic bunch. It was not likely to be a problem.

*Pamela, John and I all travelled out together and were allocated
the old Station Commander's bungalow, with a well tended garden
full of exotic tropical flowers. It was a wonderful home. We also
purchased his Standard Vanguard estate for $2,000 (Singapore
dollars). (Ten Singapore dollars were worth roughly one English
guinea, £1.10.) It was a very good price for a well maintained car
and although we had upgraded the Morris 1100 to a Triumph 1300
just before I left Brampton, the Standard Vanguard was more in the
Zodiac league and was a really comfortable family car. It was good
to be back. Even the guard on the gate remembered me and after the
regulation salute greeted me with, 'Good to see you back, Sir'. I was
impressed.*

John was a typical service child and took it all in his stride; the only real change was a new amah. She adored John and in return John loved her. She would take him out to see the local Chinese shows and to visit her own family and in a very short time he was playing happily with the amah's own daughter who was of a similar age. He also developed a love of cricket, and on finding that the temperature of Singapore swimming pool water was well above freezing, decided it was much more to his liking than the temperature of the UK's outdoor pools. He was soon back into swimming and water polo and all the fun things that school swimming galas could throw at him. Pamela was also quickly back into swimming and sunbathing as well. Needless to say, I had somewhat less time for that sort of pleasurable activity!

Come to think of it, by comparison my work was pretty dour. My predecessor, an ex-Lightning pilot, stayed for a two-day hand-over then disappeared back to the UK as fast as he could go. Added to that there had been four Lightnings lost in recent months and the enquiries were all still ongoing. RAF Tengah was definitely not a happy place when we arrived.

On the plus side, Tony's team of SAF officers were a keen and receptive bunch who worked hard. However, they were very young, had a lot to learn and a relatively short time in which to be fully conversant with the many important operational tasks they were about to take over. Unfortunately, they also had to cope with a regular stream of interruptions from official SAF visitors coming by to see how they were progressing. These frequent interruptions did not help. None of the trainees had any aircrew experience and to Tony they all looked even younger than they actually were. On the plus side they were pretty bright, one having command of seven or eight languages, and all of them were happy to accept Tony and his team as 'schoolmasters'. They were all fluent English speakers and had no problems with any aspects of the technical or military English used in the Operations Room. There was a training programme in place that Tony had devised during the first four weeks of his posting, while they were waiting for their trainees to arrive. The instruction was very much hands-on and as such they were always involved in everything that was taking place in the Operations Centre; though of course they were fully supervised and never expected to make decisions on their own. There was no classwork for them to complete and no written exams for them to sit at the end of the course. The outgoing RAF team were simply left to hope that the trainees had fully understood everything that they had been shown.

The Tengah Operations Centre could be a fairly busy place from time to time. Fortunately for Tony and the rest of the team, which comprised a pilot and two Warrant Officers, one a master navigator and the other a master electronic officer, there was virtually no night flying. The Lightnings based at Tengah were almost solely on daylight operations and exercises and the Strikemasters of the embryonic Singapore Air Force were strictly on daylight operations only. It was only the odd visitor who altered that standard pattern and needed after-hours assistance. Sometimes there were visits from elements of the UK V-bomber force and of course Tengah played host to the squadrons of carrier-based Fleet Air Arm planes (Buccaneers and Sea Vixens), when the carriers returned to port at the Singapore Naval Base for re-fit, re-supply, or routine servicing. None the less, it was all pretty well regulated and Tony and the team always had the time to take part of Friday afternoon away from the Operations Room to have a meeting to talk through the following week's programme. They would also use the opportunity to allocate the work for their young SAF students, many days ahead of schedule.

The only real incident of any consequence during the whole tour was the arrival of a USAF Lockheed C5A Galaxy. It was a monster of an aircraft whose sheer size and weight put the physical capabilities of Tengah at full stretch. Empirical measurement of taxiways and hardstands covering both dimensions and its physical load-bearing capability was needed before the monster plane could be accommodated. It was a talking point across the station and in the local area for several weeks after its visit. They also lost two of the Singaporean Strikemasters during the year, both incidents were fatal and neither plane was ever found. Such were the unforgiving hazards of flying over dense jungle terrain.

We had a Corporal who ran the Operations Boards for us. He would arrive an hour before the rest of us in the morning and the whole operation was ready to be activated as soon as we arrived at eight o'clock. He always had one of the trainees with him. If one of the Singaporean chaps previously allocated to him was on holiday or off sick, we always made sure one of the others was drafted in to work on the Operations Boards; after all this would be the key to their success after we handed over to them. We also had to teach them to liaise with the local RAF radar unit, and keep track of any other non-Tengah RAF traffic. The days of multiple monitor screens keeping everyone up-to-date were still many years away. Contact with our own ATC centre was by phone.

During this time we were involved with exercises to test all aspects of operations from Tengah, ranging from a mock, full-scale attack, to sending out rescue teams to a downed crew. These exercises only occurred during the week, generally between nine in the morning and five in the afternoon, a most civilised practice that I fully endorsed. However, I had to be contactable wherever I went, and in the days before mobile phones, that meant phoning in to the duty officer and leaving a contact number if we ever went out during the evening or at the weekend.

We went on leave a few times during our stay, and revisited Penang and the Cameron Highlands, as well as spending a few days at Mersing on the eastern side of the Malaysian peninsula. We travelled to Penang by air the first time and by train the next. The Cameron Highlands trip we entrusted to the ultra-reliable Standard Vanguard estate. At Mersing, John was particularly impressed with the way the jungle came down to the sea, with just the strip of sand between its lush foliage and the water's edge. He was also taken with the quantities of monkeys that happily cavorted noisily just a few feet away from us. It was idyllic apart from the millions of sand-flies that conspired to make our time on the beach as miserable as possible.

John was by now a total water baby and into anything involving water. He joined the Marlins Swimming Club on the base. The Marlins were blessed with an excellent coach, a Sergeant PTI by calling, who soon had the youngsters training hard, entering competitions and producing some excellent performances. John responded well and was picked to represent the club at the 50-metre butterfly stroke race. By the time the end of our stay at Tengah arrived, he had *reached a standard that gained him a second place in the local Open Gala and had him regularly recording times within half a second of the local junior record.*

The social side of our life was less outgoing this time round. I was no longer aircrew, and this definitely played a part in the way our social calendar was formed. The Lightning boys were somewhat loners in their RAF role and this tended to spill over into their private and social lives. Certainly, with the dear old Canberras you always started off as a crew-based unit anyway. As well as that, we now had John to consider. We were, however, still able to host several visits by friends from the past who passed through Tengah from time to time. Keith Evans, my co-pilot from my Valiant days, was a fairly frequent and welcome visitor, as he had transferred to Transport Command and had been promoted to Captain and Squadron Leader. He was now gainfully employed ferrying RAF personnel and their dependants around the world in RAF Comets.

I still managed to play hockey on a regular basis, though I have to admit that my golf really took a back seat. For some reason I found it easier to play two, thirty-minute halves of energetic hockey, than a fairly gentle stroll round the golf course for three hours. I suspect it was nothing to do with the energy expended, rather it was a straight comparison between the two half-hour playing periods with a refreshment break and the straight three hours out in the hot sun, non-stop.

We also had some very enjoyable encounters with the Changi and Raffles Hockey Club. Being Hindu, they provided a curry for the refreshment break and we supplied the beer; it seemed like a fair exchange. Their religion forbade the drinking of alcohol, but somehow they always seemed to get a dispensation when they visited us.

As the end of his tour approached, the intensity of the visits by Singaporean civil servants increased as they monitored the progress of their young team. Their instruction squad had never put them under any real pressure, but by the time the RAF were ready to leave, the instructors were pretty confident their fledglings were up to the job. Tony's team had frequently experienced the somewhat frosty attitude of the Malaysian Airspace Authority, but had shown their trainees how to deal with the Malaysian reluctance to allow SAF aircraft to over-fly their territory. It was essential they mastered this diplomatic hurdle as Singapore airspace was very limited and Indonesian airspace a total no-go area for them.

The departure of the last squadron of Lightnings occasioned the final major RAF parade at Tengah, shortly after which the Victor tankers arrived, ready to ferry the Squadron back to the UK. The Squadron's departure was poignant and following the obligatory, non-approved, low-level beat up by the last plane to take off, an eerie silence descended over the airfield. Somehow, to Tony and his team, the later sound of the SAF Strikemasters was not the same, and it was obvious that this outpost of the old British Empire was finally closing down.

Pamela and John were scheduled out on one of the Comets that were now making regular trips between Singapore and Changi taking home dependants and non-essential personnel. They would be heading to Pamela's parents in Cleethorpes, where I would join them for the Christmas break. By the time they departed for home I knew I had about two weeks left before I, too, was to return to the UK, so I moved out of the bungalow and into the Mess – it seemed the most sensible thing to do. I sold the trusty Vanguard to one of the Australian pilots who was training the SAF crews on their Strikemasters. I was very sad to see it go. I got back what I had paid for it and throughout my year of ownership, had bought just three replacement re-mould tyres and mended one puncture. That had to be the cheapest and most reliable motoring I had ever had in my entire life.

I had already been informed that my next posting was a return to Victor tankers and RAF Marham, but a serious refresher course in navigation would be needed before I made it back on to a squadron. Three years away from regular flying was bound to make any navigator rusty, and there were naturally new bits of kit and techniques to get to grips with. I was looking forward to it all. In the meantime I had two rather long and quiet weeks to get through before repatriation. My SAF chaps had left with little ceremony, a slightly formal 'thank you', a salute and a brisk handshake brought their year's training and my usefulness at Tengah to an end.

A couple of weeks later, the Station CO, G/Cpt Peter Latham, popped his head round my office door.

'Thanks Tony, your job's completed here. Well done. Let's get you on a plane home.'

I was moving on again.

CHAPTER 8

Finningley, Marham and the Victor Mk 1

ourse 227 at No. 6 FTS (Flying Training School) Finningley
was designated a refresher course, which indeed it was,
but it also had a very thorough syllabus and was not to be
treated as an easy trip, even for guys who should have remembered
most of it anyway. It covered everything from the basics, through
the systems the students had been used to operating on their
previous postings, to some of the new procedures and kit they
would be encountering when they arrived at their new squadrons,
some time after the Christmas break. That however, was still a
couple of months away. Several weeks of ground school had to be
completed and passed before they could take their places in the
de Havilland Dominies used by Finningley for the airborne part of
the course. That said, the whole procedure was less formal than
previous courses, in that as long as the work was completed and
done to a reasonable standard, then strict adherence to office hours
was not always necessary. In fact, providing all was well, then the
course instructors were happy for students to finish for the week
at lunchtime on the Friday, and they rarely had anything planned
before lunch on the following Monday. That gave everyone
the opportunity to stay in the Mess mid-week and go home for the
weekend and have some reasonable semblance of home life. This

all led to a very comfortable and mature atmosphere on the course, where everything was done correctly and on time, and everyone benefited from a more relaxed regime.

Tony and his friend and travelling companion Ron Higgins took advantage of this and used the Monday morning and Friday afternoons to commute up and down the A1 between Houghton and Finningley. As the Higgins and Golds families lived within half a mile of each other, it was most convenient. Also it enabled Ron's VW Caravanette to be used for the run, and for Pamela to have the recently acquired Golds family Ford Cortina, as her Triumph 1300 had started to play up with a series of niggling problems.

Even the Dominies contributed to this rather civilised ambience. Firstly they were a really sophisticated aircraft in every sense of the word, being the military version of the airframe developed from the civil Hawker Siddley HS 125 Executive Jet. It was pressurised, had full temperature control, a loo, coffee-making equipment and an ultra-rapid start-up sequence that allowed the students to be finishing a coffee in the Crew Room, and a mere five minutes later be strapped in and taxiing towards the runway holding point, ready for take-off. How good was that! It also had a much larger working area for the navigator than any other plane Tony had encountered before. Add to that the lighter weight personal kit, flying suits, radio mikes and headphones, and you can easily see the attraction. These points alone gained the praise of every navigator who stepped foot in one.

The students were paired together for the airborne section of the course and that worked out really well. I frequently operated with Ron or with Derek Aldridge, both were good chaps to have with you on these time-critical training sorties. The Dominie had a duration of about three and a quarter hours and frequently our training exercises were planned to take the full three hours. There was little room for the odd excursion away from the ideal route, and it was very handy to have a second set of knowledgeable eyes watching the clock. Besides that, our pilots who flew these sorties on a regular basis, would soon get a bit twitchy if we took too long to sort ourselves out after turning at a waypoint. After all, it was their responsibility to get the plane home regardless of any SNAFU (airman's speak –

The Avro Anson used to give apprentices air experience. 'C' Squadron, 70th Entry, in all their glory.

The boys of 'C' Squadron. Tony and chums, Denyer, Miles and Spencer.

RAF Locking ... 'swotting' – Yeah, right!

'C' Squadron having time off. Tony plus Denyer, Miles, Hitchins and Spencer.

Officer Cadets at Cirencester, 1957.

No. 139 COURSE 'A' FLIGHT
BAKER BARRETT-JOLLEY BATES BROOKS CARTER
COLLIS CRAWFORD CROSBY-CLARKE DAWSON DELANEY
DUFF FITZGERALD FORSTER GARDUTT GONES GREEN

Officer Training. Cirencester, 1957.

No. 1 Navigation School, Topcliffe, 1960.

189 Canberra Conversion Course OCU Bassingbourn.

Tony Golds' first love ... the Canberra B2. With Pilot Officer Butler. Butterworth to Tengah, 15-06-62.

Tengah 61/62 RAF Hockey team. Gus Ross (left of goalkeeper) and Tony Golds (kneeling in front of Goalkeeper). (Monty was a squash player.)

Operation *Joss Stick*. Jimmy Milne, Gus Ross, Tony Golds and their USAF host.

Operation *Joss Stick*.

Victor to Victor. Perfect refuelling alignment.

A Russian Tupolev. 'Our' Lightning took this on a Tansor sortie.

Valiant to Valiant refuelling.

Valiant to Vulcan – Perfect alignment.

Victor to Vulcan refuelling. Another foot or two lower and this Vulcan probe would have become a Mess trophy, mounted on a wooden plinth!

Marham overhead, late evening.

Home! Victor K1 landing at Marham – chute deployed.

Victor plus Tornados. Overhead Marham, 06 threshold.

Victor 'Fuel flowing'.

The end of a Victor at RAF Marham (Prior to Tansor exercise). Note the ejection seat doing just that to the left of the smoke column. All the crew (not Tony's) escaped. Tony was in the Ops room at the time ... having a very busy day.

Formal 'boy's night out' RAF Marham . . . any year between 1980 and 1990 (take your pick!).

Victor Mk.II to Vulcan, pre *Black Buck*. Practise to get the big day right.

C130 Closing.

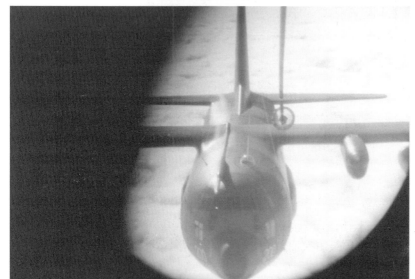

C130 Getting closer.

C130. Contact –
Pushing – Green light
on – Fuel flowing.

A part of Wideawake apron. A very busy place during the Falkland War and the year(s) that followed. Fixed and rotary wing aircraft mixed with tons of freight and equipment.

Home sweet home?

Victor showing off at Wideawake. Three drogues trailing, Port wingtip vortex was blowing up dust. That's low!

Year		AIRCRAFT		Pilot	Aircrew Duty
Month	Date	Type & Mk.	No.		Totals brought forward
—	—	—	—	—	
MAY	1	VICTOR K2	XL231		NAVIGATOR
MAY	1	VICTOR K2	XL231		NAVIGATOR
MAY	4	VICTOR K2	XL231		NAVIGATOR
MAY	5	VICTOR K2	XL231		NAVIGATOR
MAY	6	VICTOR K2	XL158		NAVIGATOR
MAY	2	VICTOR K2	XL158		NAVIGATOR
MAY	8	VICTOR K2	XL231		NAVIGATOR
MAY	10	VICTOR K2	XH675		NAVIGATOR
MAY	12	VICTOR K2	XL163		NAVIGATOR
MAY	15	VICTOR K2	XL232		NAVIGATOR
MAY	18	VICTOR K2	XL158		NAVIGATOR
MAY	22	VICTOR K2	XL192		NAVIGATOR
MAY	25	VICTOR K2	XL158		NAVIGATOR
MAY	26	VICTOR K2	XL189		NAVIGATOR
MAY	27	VICTOR K2	XL189		NAVIGATOR
MAY	29	VICTOR K2	XH669		NAVIGATOR
MAY	30	VICTOR K2	XH669		NAVIGATOR
MAY	31	VICTOR K2	XH675		NAVIGATOR

SON. LDR
NAV. PLOT. LDR.

SON. LDR
FLT. CMDR
NO 55 SON.

SUMMARY FOR MAY 1982

UNIT NO. 55 SQN.

DATE 8 JUNE 1982

SIGNATURE

Totals carried forward

Log Book pages. Some of the first Falklands War entries for the Elliott crew.

Flight Details	Day (1)	Night (2)	Captain (3)	Spare (4)
	2789 40	7302 0	3420 00	
MAR - BOSCOMBE DOWN	0.45			
B.D - MARHAM	0.30			
T.A.T.	2.30			
CORPORATE	3.55			
CORPORATE		2.55		
R.A.9		1.30		
CORPORATE	2.55	2.30		
R.A.7	3.05			
R X TRG.		1.45		
A.A.R.	2.05			
CORPORATE		4.05		
R.X. TRG	6.15			
CORPORATE	3.30	2.00		
R.A.7	3.40	3.15		
CORPORATE	2.50	4.00		
CORPORATE	3.50			
COR POR ATE	3.55			
CORPORATE	4.20			
VICTOR K 2.	44.05	22.00		
GRAND TOTAL. 811.25.				
	28 33.45	7622 0	3586.05	

55 Squadron Farewell Parade. Well
drilled airmen form the final parade.

Tony and Maryse at
home in Boughton.

Tony and Maryse. Walking in
the Lake District.

'situation normal, all fouled up') that the students made during the exercise. Fortunately none occurred with Course 227.

Early in November it was time to brush the dust off the cover of my log book as we started our brief association with the Dominie, and its rather comfortable non-military features. After the familiarisation flight in XS732 on Tuesday 2 November, we got stuck into the bulk of the training exercises. By the 22nd we were into the night aspect of the course and by the 26th we headed off on the final big trip; a fun couple of days in Gibraltar, with a navex (navigation exercise) planned via Porto in northern Portugal on the way out and a navex via Nice on the way back on the 29th. So with that completed and with twenty-seven and a quarter hours logged in the Dominie, I headed back to Norfolk, Marham and the Victors of 232 OCU.

Tony joined Course 99, 232 OCU Marham and resumed his Nav/Plotter seat in a Victor tanker on 3 February 1972. The pattern of his life was the same as the early JARIC days, spending weekends at home and living in the Mess during the week, with a couple of hours commuting between the two. Of course, this time home was near Huntingdon and work was in Norfolk. Needless to say, this was only temporary and the house soon went on the market, as the recent housing boom put the Golds' finances in a very comfortable position for the purchase of the next family home. Tony's economics lecturer at Cambridge had advised him to keep the house during the Tengah posting and rent it out for the year. His view was that house prices would sky-rocket during that time. They did, though even he could not have foreseen quite how much the Golds' home in Houghton and Wyton would appreciate in such a short time.

February and the first week of March at 232 OCU were incredibly busy for all the aircrew passing through. Tony's log book recorded a total of fifty-six hours and ten minutes for the month, with twenty-five hours logged at night; all on 232 OCU's Victor Mk 1s. He then had a couple of weeks' leave, and on his return in April headed across the Marham apron to 214 Squadron and its fleet of Victor K1s.

The first two months on 214 Squadron involved acclimatisation exercises to mould the new boys back into the swing of Squadron life. The K1s themselves were very similar to the earlier Mk 1s, so that was no real problem, but there was some additional navigational kit to get used to. Fortunately, it had all been added to make the navigator's life easier. However, by Tuesday 13 June, the training was over and Tony was back on the Squadron strength and fully integrated into the team.

Secondary duties arrived with my Squadron locker key. I was able to take on my favourite duty, that of Station hockey representative. My other secondary duty was not quite so appealing, I was put in charge of No. 3 Hangar. Thus all minor repairs, broken windows, light bulbs that failed and plumbing that went AWOL were all part of my remit. In itself that was not too bad, but of course, as with all military functions such as this, there came the regulation inspections. Being the officer in the firing line, this meant that immediately before the Station CO's inspection, the Squadron Commander wanted one of his own to make sure it was all in order for the big day. Obviously, there was no way I was going into a Squadron Commander's inspection blind, so I did my own just prior to this, checking to ensure all reported damage was repaired and the whole of my area was as it should be. You can see from this, that the week before the big day was a pretty busy time and fully dedicated to checks and inspections.

All flight crews were also allocated duties in the Operations Centre. Mine included checking crew records and chasing up the guys to ensure their medical profiles were up to speed, with all their checks, tests and jabs completed in due time. I was amazed at the number of really feeble excuses, regularly put forward by grown men, to explain the reason why they had not yet visited the Station Medical Centre.

I did just one trip in May then headed off to Majorca with the family for two glorious weeks in the sun. We took a holiday package out of Luton to Palma, where John renewed his on-off-on relationship with water and swimming. The temperature of the Mediterranean in May was very much to his liking. So much so that we still had to keep an eye on him when the sun was at its height, and bring him into the shade and apply sun lotion. The food was great and there was a well organised programme of events for both children and adults.

June was very much a case of 'back to work' with the memory of the holiday fading as fast as the suntan, and with Tony flying pretty regularly with the F/Lt 'Banfy' Banfield crew. They regularly refuelled the Lightnings that were scrambled to intercept the ultra long-range, Russian Air Force Tupolev TU144s bombers (NATO code name Bear). The Tupolevs came round over the top of Sweden and Norway, across the Northern Atlantic and down the Eastern Seaboard of America on their way to Cuba. The RAF, using the Lightnings, took over tracking the heavy bombers from the Swedish Air Force and covered the North Sea to Iceland stretch of the Tupolev's route. They in turn handed over to the US Air Force who were stationed in Iceland, who then monitored the Russian planes all the way down to the Caribbean with their F15s. There was a nice break towards the end of the month for Tony and the crew of XA938 as they were assigned a three-day trip to Cyprus with a very pleasant, sunny, two-day stopover at Akrotiri.

July 1972 was a month like any other for Tony, but upon reflection it was a bit of a red letter month. On 10 July, halfway through a training exercise in XA936 with S/Ldr McDougall (The Laird), Tony's log passed the 2,000-hour mark. His log entry noted five hours twenty minutes for the trip, but nothing else. Perhaps the casualness of passing such a landmark was due to the fact that he was also flying for the next three days on the trot with two Lightning refuelling sorties and a flying reunion with his old chum Jeremy Price. He flew with Jeremy again in August and in September, then stayed with 'Banfy' for most of the remainder of September, including the weeklong exercise 'Strong Express'. That was a very intensive phase of flying in a short period of time for anyone. Fortunately, the schedule for October worked out the complete opposite and he only had three sorties. November was again fairly busy, then in December, just as they were all thinking of Christmas leave and the holiday period, he had the opportunity to fly in XH667, one of the new Victor K2Ps. Thus on 15 December he logged a two hours forty minutes, K2, Towline sortie with F/Lt Barrett.

The K2 was a different beast than the older Mk 1s. Although to the casual onlooker it had a basically similar profile, it was visually different in many respects and vastly different in several others under the skin, especially with regards to the power of the engines. The power was awesome compared with the earlier models and the Crew Room gossip was that it was so good, that the aircraft could perform almost as well on three engines as it did on four. Certainly, the talk was that the loss of an engine would not automatically cause the abandonment of an operation, as was almost certain with the Mk 1. He had one more flight on 19 December, but unfortunately that was aborted after just half an hour due to an aircraft fault, then ... holiday time.

We had Christmas in Downham Market where Pamela and I had bought a small bungalow on Hillcrest. We had also bought a piece of land at Boughton, a few miles outside Downham, where we were having a house built to our specification and design. The reason we were able to afford to do this was because we had earlier taken the advice of my economics lecturer at Cambridge and had not sold the house in Houghton when we departed for Tengah. We had rented it out, and exactly as predicted by my lecturer, its value had almost trebled in the twelve months we were away. We had enough surplus cash from that sale to build the new house and still buy the place on Hillcrest as a temporary home. We also upgraded the Golds family transport at the same time. I had a BMW 2002 and Pamela, who by now was back at work, had a Cortina 2000E.

John had passed his eleven plus exam and had settled down well at Downham Market Grammar School. In the absence of a warm water swimming pool he had abandoned swimming again and taken to fishing and horse riding, and like most boys his age, greatly enjoyed playing football and cricket at school. There were no prizes for guessing where he inherited his love of sports. Our social life continued to be most enjoyable and our weekend calendar was always pretty full. However, the impending move to Boughton was about to put a real block on John's social life as Boughton, delightful a village as it was, was totally dead and unexciting for a lively twelve-year-old, more adapted to busy town and RAF station life.

The new house started to take shape and I visited the site almost every Friday afternoon. My wellingtons lived permanently in the boot of the BMW. I regularly mooched around the site, trying to monitor progress, dressed in uniform and wellies. The building

process seemed very slow, but the local family firm of Covell and
Son, who were doing the work, were very thorough and reliable. It
was well worth the wait. Needless to say, we planned to go on a
spending spree when we moved into the new house, having decided
that almost everything in it would be new. That, however, was over
a year or more away. 1973 was now upon us.

The highlight for the 'Banfy' crew in January 1973 was a three-
day trip to RAF Gütesloh. For Tony the February highpoint was
another trip in a Mk 2, this time with W/Cdr Skingsley, again
in XH667. March was pretty routine except for a RTB (Return to
Base) on the 26th, when XA927's alternator failed. On the 30th,
Tony headed south with the Brunton crew, back to one of his old
favourite places, Cyprus, for a few days. They flew some Phantoms
out to Akrotiri and then undertook a refuelling operation on
4 April before returning to Marham on 5 April. They had a lot of
spare time on that trip, and Tony took the opportunity to meet up
again with members of the Riding Club at Akrotiri and spent a lot
of his off duty hours on horseback in the glorious spring sunshine.

If April had been quiet for Tony, then May was hectic. From 15
to 17 May he returned to the Mediterranean with the Barrett crew,
to Malta; then on 25 May he was back with the Banfield crew and
heading out across the Atlantic to the USA. They had been chosen
to be part of the team responsible for the tanker-proving flights
from the UK to the west coast of America, non-stop. This was all in
preparation for Operation 'Red Flag'.

It took Victor tanker XA932 a total of nine hours and twenty-five
minutes to fly from RAF Marham in Norfolk to USAF Offutt
in Nebraska. They stayed there for a couple of days, then returned
home at a more leisurely pace, via the more conventional route
through Goose Bay and Gander in Newfoundland on the Eastern
seaboard of Canada. The final hop across the Atlantic was on
1 April back to Marham and took just four hours and forty minutes.
The crew all added eighteen hours and fifty-five minutes to their
log books for that one. This was Tony's first experience of tanker
proving flights ... it would not be his last.

July and August were both filled with refuelling sorties, though I did
manage one Malta trip with F/Lt Uprichard.

November was a bit busy for Tony with multiple refuelling sorties and several days on loan to the OCU, which entailed a couple of overnight stops at Leuchars and Wattisham. The positioning flights after the overnighters were fun, with just forty minutes for the Leuchars to Marham leg and a mere twenty for the Wattisham to Marham hop. He had just three sorties in December, including his first Harrier refuelling trip on the 17th. This brought his year to an end and, looking back, it had certainly been different. There were some moments that, sadly, were unlikely to be repeated and others he would make doubly sure he would never knowingly repeat again. 1974 was looking favourable.

The new year had a very slow start. I had just three trips in January and two in February, though one was a rather interesting tanker-to-tanker refuelling sortie on the 18th. Unsurprisingly, you became much more conscious of a very large Victor just a few feet behind your tail, rather than the more diminutive, by comparison, fighters that we were normally asked to service.

March was busier with a week's sortie back to Tengah and a delightful two-day stopover in Gan, which gave me an excellent chance to top-up my fading suntan.

April saw another two trips in one of the long-awaited Victor K2s. We were frequently told that the days of all K2 tanker operations was getting closer, but it seemed to be taking an age to fully equip the Squadron. The K2 appeared again in June and I had three trips in XH667, though they were all short tests or check-outs. There was then a three-month 'K2 gap' in my log. All my log book entries showed Mk 1s until 18 October, when I had the chance to get back in a K2 with W/Cdr Sills.

If October was quiet, then November more than made up for it, including a two-day participation for a Lightning squadron's TACEVAL with my old team, the 'Banfy' crew. The TACEVAL was a training exercise like no other and deserves a bit of explanation. A full station TACEVAL is explained in detail a little later, as it was a strange exercise, being both far removed from our normal day-to-day operations, yet also being the main situation that the RAF were training for. This one in November was merely to assist the evaluation of the Lightning's station readiness. It was nowhere near as stressful for us as a TACEVAL at our own Station.

December finished off a fairly routine year with a few trips back to Luqa and some winter sunshine in the Mediterranean. Also around this time we lost my good chum 'Banfy' to the pleasures and delights of the Battle of Britain Memorial Flight (BBMF). He was no doubt one of the best men for the job, but would be greatly missed on the Squadron. Christmas 1974 was to be our last in Downham Market as the construction of our new house at Boughton was making steady progress towards completion and would be ready for occupation towards the end of the following year (1975).

Unsurprisingly, Tony returned to Luqa again in January, and then again in April. He completed some ground school revision at Marham and in the same month some skiing in and around Aviemore in Scotland during this quiet time, to compensate for not flying. The ground school was not that thrilling, but the skiing was a most acceptable diversion.

May was busy with a fairly balanced mixture of operations and exercises, including several refuelling operations with a number of naval aircraft (Phantom F4s). But June was all change and the first week saw a return to the USA on a very long-distance refuelling exercise back to Offutt in Nebraska. Going out in two legs over two days was no real problem, but the return trip from Offutt to Marham in one hop with a flight time of nine hours and five minutes, was a long-haul operation in anyone's book. July was quiet and time for a spot of leave, as the long-awaited course at 232 OCU, for conversion on to the Mk 2, was scheduled for August, September and the first two weeks of October. It also enabled Tony to meet up again with Jeremy Price, now sporting all the costume jewellery of a Wing Commander on his uniform. Jeremy had been appointed CO of 232 OCU along with his new rank.

It came as little surprise to me that Jeremy had progressed this far. It had always been obvious he was destined for higher things. He was a superb pilot, meticulous in his pre-flight preparation, and a great team player. He was a competent leader and displayed all the attributes needed in an RAF officer with all the potential to hold his own in the rarefied atmosphere of the upper reaches of the Air Force.

Once again, at the OCU, the pattern of RAF conversion courses repeated itself. The aircrews faced several weeks in the classroom, both refreshing basic knowledge and learning the theory of their new equipment, followed by a couple of intensive flying weeks converting to the new aircraft and its kit, in the air. It was good to fly with Jeremy on my last flight with the OCU in XL233. Now I was off across the Marham apron yet again, this time to 55 Squadron.

CHAPTER 9

More Marham and the Victor Mk 2

The Victor Mk 2 was a natural evolution of the Victor One, except in the engine department where it was more of a revolution. The extra power available from the Mk 2's Rolls-Royce Conway 201 engines was just phenomenal compared with that available to its more genteel forebear. The dear old Mk 1 had just 44,000 pounds of thrust to lift it off the ground, whereas the Mk 2 had all of 82,400 pounds of thrust to do the same job. Needless to say, from the crew's perspective, even with an additional fuel load for increased duration, the new Victor K2s fairly leapt off the ground. From a navigator's point of view, it meant that everything had to be pinned down or locked in place prior to take-off or it rolled or slid to the back of the table during the climb.

I remember it was a great time for me. There was the new plane, the new Squadron and a new house all arriving at much the same time. We had been given a moving in date for December, so the Golds family Christmas 1975 would be at Boughton. We put our cottage in Hillcrest in the hands of an estate agent, anticipating and getting, a quick sale as the housing market was booming. We planned the new furniture, the new fixtures and fittings and the house-warming party all at the same time. I had designed the place myself, basing it unashamedly around our pretty active social life. I had hired a local architect to draw up the plans for me and to make sure I had not made any basic mistakes from a building and planning perspective. We had also hoped to have our own swimming pool, but sadly that was the one aspect of luxury living that never quite made it from the drawing board to the site. We did have the house offset in the plot for this reason, and even to this day, there is a very large lawn covering the area of garden where I had always planned to have the pool.

Despite these changes on the domestic front, in reality nothing much changed work-wise. By 6 January I was back in the air, this time for a sortie with the Lovett crew, with whom I would spend many months during the next year. It was a Phantom and Buccaneer refuelling exercise, and the forerunner of a series of training exercises leading up to a two-day Joint Maritime Exercise with the Royal Navy, refuelling some of their carrier-based squadrons.

February was very quiet on the flying front, as I continued my usual habit of using a couple of weeks' annual leave around this time every year, to go on a skiing break to Scotland. Over the years I managed to become quite proficient at skiing, and enjoyed outings at Aviemore, Glenshee and most of the Scottish winter resorts. This year would be no exception. However, as they say, no good deed ever goes unpunished, and boy did I pay for those two weeks of fun when I returned to the Squadron in March. It started on the second of the month and finally finished on the thirtieth. Eleven operations, seven pilots, thirty-nine hours airborne, with just over thirty of them at night and, to cap it all, most of them as part of a competition against the USAF. There was a great deal of pre-flight preparation needed, usually about one and a half hours on the ground to one hour in the air. When you add to that the fact that we were on 100 per cent oxygen from the start of each flight, it was easy to see why we were all pretty tired at the end of the competition.

There were three more competition tasks slotted into the first week of April. It took to 12 April for the Lovett crew to return to some semblance of standard operations. I really did feel that their lordships in the Ministry had squeezed their full money's worth out of me for that particular month's salary cheque. I then had just one week of normality in which to prepare for a quick run down to the Med, to

the spring sunshine of Malta and RAF Luqa ... perhaps it was not
so bad after all, all things considered.

The highlight of May for the Lovett crew was a return to the
United States to Offutt and the long-distance tanker escort for
the fighters going out to the west coast of America. They flew the
Marham to Goose Bay sector on 20 May, the Goose to Offutt
sector on 21 May, then had a few days of the renowned USAF
hospitality in Omaha, until the return home late on 24 May. This
time the socialising included hiring a car and motoring around
in the Omaha area taking in all the tourist sights, as well as taking
up the many invitations for drinks, BBQs and parties that were
always arranged on their arrival. This aspect of the American trips
would, however, soon be changing, as the need for greater security
around their operations kicked in with the advent of the trans-
atlantic trips of the V-bomber force.

They had the benefit of a really good tail wind on that return trip
(Offutt direct to Marham) and were home in just eight hours and
ten minutes, landing at Marham an hour and a half after darkness
had fallen. By then Tony only had two more trips with 55 Squadron,
as on 14 June he and the members of several of the more experienced crews in the Squadron were reassigned to add strength and
experience to the newly formed 57 Squadron.

The first trip with my new Squadron was with my new Squadron
Leader, S/Ldr Beer (later to become an Air Vice-Marshal and equerry
to the Royal Household). In July I flew once more with my old
chum Jeremy Price, who was still very much a hands-on CO, despite
sporting the rank of Wing Commander.

August was again time for the usual family holiday and so July
and August added only a little over twenty-five hours to my log book
between them. However, as seemed to be the pattern of my flying
career, the month following any sort of break was a real heavyweight
one. September 1976 was no exception. For that month I added over
forty hours to my log book, which was now very rapidly nearing
3,000 hours. That magic figure came midway through a Buccaneer
refuelling operation on 28 October in XL192. In true Marham
tradition it went completely unnoticed.

Our second Christmas at Boughton was looming in the distance and the flying workload was not so great, although secondary duties always kept everyone with plenty to do. I was no exception. I was for ever being surprised by how many bits of a hangar could fail or need repairing during the course of a year, and how many things just 'happened' around the site, without a single person seeing or hearing anything. In late December I could, however, shut my mind to it all for a few days over the Christmas and enjoy the company of the guys on the Squadron and their ladies, as well as my own family and friends from around the Downham Market, Marham and Boughton areas. Added to that, I only had just over six weeks or so to wait until my next skiing expedition and by now John was joining me on these Scottish trips, as he had recently added skiing to his ever growing repertoire of sporting accomplishments. Around this time I also became involved with some of the local charitable organisations in Downham Market, starting when I joined the Lions Club. This gave me a passing involvement with the Round Table and the local Rotary Club; all worthwhile organisations that I felt I could work with and support.

My hockey year had also been successful, and I had managed to secure a place in the third team of the local hockey club, The Pelicans, based in King's Lynn. Squadron cricket had also gone rather well; not that that was a surprise to anyone. With Jeremy Price as both opening bat and a first-class bowler, we secured the Station Aircrew Cup with what seemed like indecent ease. I have to point out that Jeremy was also opening bat for the Bomber Command eleven and would often put as many runs on the score card as the rest of us put together. Understandably, a team of one player, however good, was not acceptable under the rules of cricket, so we lesser mortals all got a game.

John had settled down, more or less, in Boughton, but it was deadly dull for him. He soon took to fishing, horse riding and joined the local Sea Scouts. His ability on a horse was as good as his ability on skis. For the skiing I needed to head off a week ahead of him in order to be at his standard when he arrived! His equestrian skills were at a similarly high level and whilst I had frequent discussions with my mount about who was in charge and which way we were to go, John would simply leap on board, pat the horse on the neck and *canter off into the distance. He also met his first proper girlfriend about the same time – real serious stuff for a lad in his early teens. The Mum and Dad Taxi Company was soon pressed into regular service. With my commitment to Marham, Pamela's new job with the Registry Office in Downham and the family taxi requirements, coupled to the remoteness of Boughton and its complete lack of bus services, the cars were a very hard pressed and essential part of our daily life. However, John's busy life really demanded an alternative means of transport, so as soon as he was old enough, he became the proud owner of a 50cc Honda. This served him well and gave Pamela and me good notice of his return home in the evenings. We could hear its buzzing several miles out from home, as he made his way along the Norfolk lanes on his way back to Boughton. He kept it for quite a while until the self-inflicted 'Honda Rash' became a far too frequent occurrence, as the little machine spat him off onto the gravel on the side of the road.*

For Tony, 1977 started much as previous years; the first three months followed the standard Golds' New Year pattern. A gentle start in January, skiing and little else in February, then headfirst into March and a busy three months rushing into the summer that gave him hardly any time for anything else, other than work. He flew with S/Ldr Dick Hayward on his return from skiing in February and from then on for most of the following year he was pretty much part of the Hayward crew.

Thirty-three hours in March, twenty-seven in April and nearly twenty-five in May was a pretty solid workload for the spring of 1977, particularly if you take into account the fact it included operations to Akrotiri, Luqa, a TACEVAL at RAF Leuchars and a couple of TANSOR (Tanker Sortie) support refuelling sorties heading north to assist with the intercept of the Russian Bears.

It was on one of these TANSOR exercises that they nearly lost one of the Phantoms they were supposed to be refuelling. The Phantom pilot was relatively inexperienced and became carried away and fixated with the shadowing part of his mission and presumably forgot about the need to refuel. The Russian Tupolev had descended to low level and the Phantom had dropped down to follow him. Tony's Victor, however, was in its correct position and at its standard operating height of 30,000 feet when he started calling the Phantom and sending out the locator signals. Unbeknown to him at the time, there was something like a 28,000 feet altitude difference between them. For nearly an hour Tony kept calling on the radio and pressing the transmit button before the pilot of the receiver plane appeared for his life saving refuelling session; however, not before he had been forced to jettison all his rockets and missiles to lighten his aircraft sufficiently to make the *rendezvous*. The guess was that he was just about running on fumes when the probe locked in.

I was very glad it was not me at the receiving end of the particular interview with the Station Commander that would surely have followed that occurrence. The chance of a Board of Inquiry, following the 'loss' of ordnance at a cost of several thousands of pounds a time, must have been a real possibility. His only mitigation was that he did eventually returned the plane refuelled, back to base in one piece.

My workload for September was over thirty-eight hours, and October was thirty-two. No guessing then, that I had been on leave during August and this was payback time again. I would point out in my defence that July had also been a thirty-two-hour month, but that seemed to make little difference to the post-leave pattern of work. My guess was that it was the same for all of us as we covered for other aircrew taking leave.

September had included a 'Red Flag' exercise back to Offutt, quickly followed by a week operating out of Akrotiri again, so even I had to admit that the enjoyment side really did balance the long hours. One more trip with the Hayward crew to Offutt was my only operation in December and it brought 1977 to a close. I knew then that, for a while at least, my flying days were to go on hold again, as in March I was heading for the Marham Operations Room for a ground tour. I had just three more flights in January and three in February to finish things off, so when XH675 touched down on the Marham runway in the late evening of 28 February, I became a 'desk-wallah' again.

CHAPTER 10

Operations at Marham

I was scheduled to have a further couple of weeks' leave after I had returned from my usual, Scottish, mid-winter skiing trip, prior to claiming my desk in the Operations Centre at Marham. That just didn't happen; I was asked to come in early as one of the guys I was to replace had been posted before his scheduled time and the workload needed two officers to cover the shift periods, due to the twenty-four hours a day, seven days a week requirement. I had popped in a day or so earlier, just for a chat with the Operations Room team I had inherited, so I knew most of them briefly. I had a team of one Sergeant, three Corporals and eight airmen who kept the Ops Boards running smoothly and the obligatory paperwork flowing.

There was no formal training course for this; I simply drove in, parked the car, walked into the office, sat down and jumped straight in at the deep end. Well, not quite ... first there was the regulation cup of coffee that was needed to start any normal Ops Room day. It was a tradition that came with the job, and one I happily passed on some years later when I relinquished it and returned to flying duties.

The team I inherited were a pretty good bunch at most things, but I do have to admit that their tea and coffee-making abilities, although acceptable most of the time, were not their strongest attributes. But then they weren't mine either, so I couldn't really get too 'chirpy' about it. Having even modest officer's jewellery on my uniform was never going to improve the quality of hastily made, instant coffee rustled up in the small area behind the Operations Boards.

103

Tony's first job was to accept the handover of all classified materials from the Classified Material Registry, which was operated by two civilians. Within the first week, he had inherited all the classified operations material and the full War Plan file. That transfer of the ops material alone took a full three days, as every document was checked against the register and then had to be almost individually signed over. During the first week Tony had familiarised himself with the various procedures associated with that elevated level of security. Within an hour or two of moving into the office, a Sergeant from the RAF Police Section came into the Operation Centre to brief him further.

Tony was aware that some had found this side of RAF duties rather onerous. Fortunately, he did not. He found it all totally straightforward and had already worked out that providing he adhered totally to the book; there was rarely a problem and certainly no comeback on him if things did go awry, providing there was a section in the book that had been strictly followed. As well as that of course, he had his JARIC experience to fall back on for the security side of things and also his year at Tengah Operations for the more day-to-day operational matters. The time spent handing over the RAF Tengah base to the emerging Singapore Air Force had been perfect training for his new job at the Marham Operations Centre.

The first major task every day was issuing the codes to the Air Electronics Officers (AEOs) for the aircraft in the Victor tanker fleet, for coordination with the V-bomber force. It was a full one-hour, highly secret procedure and was conducted in my office with the door firmly locked. Every plane had its codes allocated on a daily basis, but they were only issued to the AEO if the aircraft was going to fly. The 'old' codes were kept for two or three weeks under the same level of security, at which point Security Flight would come in, check that they were there in their entirety and take them away under lock and key, for secure disposal. I was never quite sure where they went, or who did the disposing, but once they were signed for, they were no longer under my jurisdiction. The Ops Boards were very similar to those at Tengah, except that there were sixteen of them and they carried more detailed information. When the squadrons were on an exercise and if there were several visiting aircraft about, it was not unusual to utilise all sixteen boards at once. It did get rather busy on occasions and kept us on our toes.

My week, like that of all RAF officers with Ops Room responsibility, followed a fairly standard pattern, though not always in the same order, not necessarily with the same priorities, or at the same speed. Firstly there was the weekly flying programme to plan, including latest updates on weather, aircraft serviceability and crew availability. This was a procedure that involved all of the UK front-line fighters and bombers. The UK fighter inventory at that time was pretty extensive and included Lightnings, Buccaneers, Phantoms, Jaguars, Harriers and the emerging Panavia Tornado, then in its development phase, flying out of Warton. These Tornado refuelling sorties were really the wild cards in the pack and caused me more headaches than all the rest put together. Firstly, as it was a development programme, the schedule was not always regular and usually initiated at short notice. Unsurprisingly, it could also be cancelled at even shorter notice, as the progress of the development work was totally unpredictable. The aircraft's standard refuelling run was over the Irish Sea, and as such any sortie, successful or unsuccessful, would take just over two and a half hours from take-off to landing, allowing an hour for the hook-up phase.

I then had the clearances, both military and civilian, to obtain for all the tanker operations for that day. Fortunately for my team, someone else had the job to sort the clearances for the receiver planes.

My next regular task was to preserve the security of the aircraft target codes and their updates for the V-bomber squadrons. Every time I left the room, even for a thirty-second trip to the loo, I had to lock the door. If anyone was in the room with me, they had to be ushered out to stand around in the corridor during my absence, however brief.

The War Plan Folders, Plan One and Plan Two, both had to be monitored, updated and of course kept totally secure at all times. If I was working on these, keeping them updated, then I had to be alone in the room, and the door locked from the inside.

Organising the security of visiting and diverted aircraft, and their crews' documents while they were on station, also fell into Ops Room control, as did liaising at all times with the Marham Met

Station, so that I could alert the Duty Flying Officer if any of the diversions on the day's list were weather-affected. This then involved producing the Standard Operating Procedures required for the new diversion for the affected crews. This was not quite as onerous as it seems as the RAF had twelve Master Diversion Stations and the documentation for their procedures were already known and the updates were always kept current. For visiting aircraft, as well as the security of the aircraft and its documentation, Ops were charged with looking after aircraft parking, crew accommodation, Mess facilities and all the other necessities evolving from the plane's visit.

When you add to the fact that we had to complete all the paperwork and statistics to cover the day's work, you can see both I and my team were never short of something to do. Oh, by the way, on top of this there was always the following day's flying programme to sort. There was never a dull moment and occasionally periods of barely controlled mayhem.

Whilst the majority of Tony's work covered the nine-to-five work period, there were of course night operations flown from Marham on a regular basis. There was always a two- to three-week advanced notification of any such night requirement, and as such it was usually a seamless transition from day to night operations. The procedures were all very similar and often only required a further update on weather, diversion airfield procedures and notification of crew availability. It was the latter that tended to create the headaches. Tony always started off the day with a spare crew. Inevitably, by midday they had utilised all their spare resources and from then on the rest of the day was down to juggling crews, aircraft and duties.

It was mandatory to have someone on duty in the Ops Room on a full twenty-four hour, seven days' a week basis, so whatever the time of day there was an airman available to grab the list of out-of-hours numbers and call in a team to crank the Operations Section up to full speed in a very short time.

Without these oddball call-outs, the first job of the day started around 4 am as the first signals of the day started to arrive. The airman on duty would collect and collate these and prepare them for the arrival of the team as the day's work started to unfold. The overnight section of the team would have matters in hand when the day crew arrived between 8 and 8.30 am and by 9 am the first aircraft would be ready to thunder down Marham's main runway and back into business. Obviously, during the dead of winter, the ground crews had the extra duties involved with de-icing and other cold weather procedures to carry out prior to take-off.

But then of course there was the MINEVAL and the TACEVAL. Hidden behind the RAF's love of acronyms were four days of 100 per cent, full-on, war scenario preparation exercises. Both were similar in presentation and operation, but vastly different in standing and significance.

The MINEVAL was a station-run exercise used by the Station Commander to test and check his station and its team, whereas the TACEVAL was a NATO operation that gave the final check-out that the station was prepared and ready, should a war scenario occur. In some ways the TACEVAL was a final exam where there were only two possible outcomes, pass or fail; whereas the MINEVAL was more of a mid-term set of tests, based on the end of year exam. It was set by the Station Commander, to see if and where more training and resources needed to be applied. Failure in a MINEVAL could often mean more work, revised work schedules and allocation of more or different resources. Failure in a TACEVAL went all the way to NATO and RAF/MoD Senior Command and could have very serious repercussions on any officer's career.

MINEVALs always started about three o'clock in the morning. The telephone would ring by my bedside to shatter the peace and I would be in my car, overnight bag on the back seat, and racing down the road towards Marham within five minutes. I would not have known about this in advance and as such would be unwashed, unshaven and not able to present myself in my usual tidy style. For once, arriving in perfect turnout, as if for a CO's inspection, was not what was wanted. However, as MINEVALs were irregular, but could be guaranteed to occur every four months or so, one soon learned to check the calendar and pick up the station 'vibes'. It was hard to pinpoint what day it would happen, but it was impossible not to notice that it was imminent.

When I approached the station, all hell would be let loose. All available lights would be on, klaxons would be sounding, sirens wailing and there would be sentries by the dozen, all milling about the main entrance, apparently armed to the teeth, with weapons drawn. Vehicles and men would be rushing in all directions and one could well be forgiven for imagining from the scene, that World Wars Three and Four had broken out simultaneously.

The Interrogation Team would already be on site and every detail from the speed of the phone calls and their responses, to the unlocking of the various offices and hangars would be observed and noted for the post-MINEVAL de-brief. Nothing could get started until the Ops Room was up and running. My first job was get all my codes and documents necessary to operate in wartime and head to the nuclear bunker. This involved a forty-yard dash carrying literally everything needed to operate RAF Marham at maximum effort for the next three to four days in an all-out war scenario. My team carried all they needed in secure boxes as they transferred to the one location on the base that could withstand almost anything but a direct hit. As the thick metal doors clanged shut behind us, all the sounds of the outside world that we were normally accustomed to on a day-to-day basis, just vanished in an instant. It was eerie and something you learned to live with, but never got used to. You adjusted accordingly.

Codes were needed for the bomber crews and we started to learn which crews were in, and how many were going to be available. We then had to match this with aircraft availability. We had to arrange for the aircraft to be fuelled, barriers erected for ordnance loading, guards put in place, and all personnel issued with weapons (though not live ammunition). From the outside it must have looked like total mayhem, but in reality it was actually well organised chaos.

The first three crews that arrived may well not be used to prepare the aircraft, but in all likelihood would be designated to be the first crews to become airborne and to be allocated target areas. The next crews to appear would head out to prepare as many aircraft as possible in readiness for take-off. As this was happening I was cross referencing codes and information to verify authenticity of the commands and to ensure the correct information was then passed on to the bomber and tanker crews.

In the meantime, my team checked all the other details to ensure the smooth running of the next phase of the situation – the transport for the aircrews to be taken to the Victors when needed, a quick visit to the Mess kitchens in the secure area to ensure that catering was up and running, and a check that the Medical Centre was opened, fully manned and ready to accept casualties. All the time the situation was continually updated by the Intelligence Section as the scenario unfolded for the MINEVAL.

All admin areas were evacuated and civilian staff either sent home or packed off to another area where they could carry on their work if appropriate, or simply sit and relax with a coffee as there was really nothing else they could do.

By the end of the day all the call-out procedures, for all ranks, had been fully tested and evaluated; now we moved on to day two. Overnight the aircrews had been rested, but the same did not apply to either the ground crews or to the Operations teams. We catnapped where and when we could. By now aircraft undergoing servicing and repairs were being called back into service and made ready.

Other stations likely to be affected by our MINEVAL were alerted and updated, as other parts of Marham's function within the day-to-day running of RAF had to continue; thus things like our regular refuelling sorties were routinely planned into the MINEVAL scenario. Also the TANSOR operations, supporting the surveillance of the Russian Bears, was still ongoing and could not be allowed to miss a beat.

On day two it was highly likely we could have an attack by 'terrorists' or have enemy paratroopers dropping in, to add to the complexity of the situation. On day two or three it would also be likely that some aircraft from another station would provide further confusion and mayhem by staging a mock attack on the airfield, occasionally timed to coincide with the launching of some of our own aircraft – just to make it interesting for everyone involved.

Day three was more of the same, except we were usually far more tired, but somehow ready for what came next. All our available planes were at a readiness state and the crews were by then usually falling into a pattern where they could arrange rest periods, so that safety was never compromised.

By day four most of the ground crews and security teams were wearing full Nuclear, Biological and Chemical protection equipment (NBC suits and masks). By mid-morning, all aircrews would be briefed for take-off and ferried out to their aircraft. They would then sit in the aircraft waiting and listening in for the announcement that it was time to launch.

This briefing would be given by one of three people: the Station Commander, the Wing Commander Operations, or me, as the officer running the Operations Centre at the time. Somehow, it always seemed to fall to me! A typical scenario would involve all Victors starting their engines and then dispersing around the station. Code-words would be verified for all aircraft and then issued to them.

The Tornados would be first to launch, followed by all the Victors, tankers and bombers alike. Shortly after take-off, some would return with no other duties to perform, others would complete a pre-scheduled air-to-air refuelling exercise and return, and a few would head off to carry out normal refuelling or bombing practice operations.

By late afternoon on day four it was all over. Most of the aircraft would have returned and reports were being written by all those responsible for the running of the MINEVAL. Secure documents would be returned to storage and most people would attempt to head off to bed to get some well earned rest. Unfortunately, Ops still had the following day's flying programme to prepare before they, too, could head off home.

For most of us however, the lure of sleep was much greater than the reality. Over those few days it was not unusual to emerge dehydrated, constipated, have headaches, be tired and yet still be on a high. Having lived on a total adrenalin rush for the past ninety-two hours, it usually took me another two to three days to revert to normal. Talking to my team soon after one of these four-day operations, it seemed to affect most of them the same way.

The TACEVAL was in some ways a similar operation with a few significantly different aspects. Firstly, it was a NATO-run operation and as such far more serious. If the MINEVAL was training, then the TACEVAL was real and assessed in the most minute detail. Mess up in a MINEVAL and you received a slapped wrist and everyone could learn from it. Mess up on a TACEVAL and rapid postings to remote stations where promotion and advancement chances were

*less than zero, could well be on the agenda. Your RAF career could
be over, and possibly that of the Squadron Leader or even the Wing
Commander above you. This was a situation that had to be avoided
at all costs.*

*The differences for the TACEVAL were obvious from the moment
you arrived at the gate. The NATO inspectors were there and they
stayed with you until it finished. As well as all the jobs you had to do
with a MINEVAL, if you had any sense at all, during a TACEVAL
you always made extra notes as you went along, particularly if things
got a bit sticky. Therefore, if there was ever an inquiry or anything
more formal, you had these notes available to defend your actions –
it could get that serious.*

*The other main difference was that it was far more real. For
instance, if you dispersed aircraft to other airfields, you may well
have had to send ground crews to support them. In a MINEVAL
it was sufficient to state that that was what you were doing, in a
TACEVAL you would almost certainly have to do it, even if it
meant sending several busloads of men and three or four trucks full
of essential equipment from Marham all the way to St Mawgan in
Cornwall. It had to be real and as such you had to be able to ensure
you had the transport and the facilities to look after ninety or so men
while on the move and later at the out-station. On top of that, of
course, however realistic it was, it was still an exercise, and as such
all peacetime health and safety rules still applied. We had to factor in
rest periods for the crews, monitor the state of aircraft and all the
other aspects that would come back to haunt us – and all the time
with the NATO shadow sitting beside you taking sufficient notes to
write a best seller.*

Sadly, it was during this period that the Golds' marriage really
started to unravel. Pamela had a demanding job in the Registry
Office in Downham Market, which was increasingly absorbing
more of her energies and attention. Operations at RAF Marham,
whilst easily within Tony's capabilities, was never going to be a
nine-to-five job that could be done on auto-pilot. Almost inevitably
they drifted apart. They still held frequent house parties and kept
up a front that all was well, but it could not stay like that for
ever. Eventually, Pamela made the decision that they were both

inevitably waiting for, and announced that she wanted a divorce. They were both becoming aware that their lives were heading in separate directions and there seemed little that could be done to change things. Tony's reaction was almost one of relief. So without a fight, it was then just a matter of time for the lawyers to do their work and the sad business of sorting out the final details.

For Tony, the financial side was initially a nightmare as he had already made up his mind to keep the house at Boughton. This would be a crushing financial commitment that would take nearly two years to stabilise. There was a sudden rapid change of lifestyle as bills and creditors' requirements took preference over Mess bills, parties and all the trappings that had been an integral part of the Golds' lifestyle up to then.

By December 1979 the divorce was through and he was a single man again. On the brighter side of things, by the time his posting in Operations was through at the beginning of 1981, he had met Maryse and it was obvious to him that she would feature heavily in his life from then on.

They would be married in October 1981, but before that there was a new posting back to tankers on 55 Squadron and the ground school, retraining and revision flights to complete at 232 OCU that were associated with the move.

CHAPTER 11

Back to 55 Squadron and the Falklands

For Tony it was again 'back to school' before returning to 55 Squadron. Three years away from squadron flying and the RAF system deemed that he needed a full refresher course before he flew operationally on tankers again, and so the early part of 1981 was spent back at RAF Finningley with 348 Navigation Revision Course. The pattern was much as before on previous revision courses, with several weeks of ground school to get through before they were allowed back aboard the Finningley fleet of Dominies for some real navigation exercises and flying.

Amazingly, on my second week on the Dominies I was reunited with XS732, an aircraft I had first flown in some ten years earlier on refresher Course 227. I did the first of my night astro navigation sorties aboard XS732 on this latest course, then went on to XS710 for the second and finally on to XS730 for the remainder of the course, which included an interesting two-day trip to Gatow in Berlin, for an overnight stopover in that historic, but divided, city. That away trip started to make me feel that I was once again getting back into the world that I knew and loved.

It was then some more ground school on Course 19 with 232 OCU at Marham then again on to the K2 at the end of August for an eight-week refresher on the Victor and all it had to offer. There was nothing really new, so the eight weeks passed pretty uneventfully, even though the workload was high with over sixty-three hours flown before the course was concluded. This time round I was beginning to realise that I was not as young as I used to be. Also, although still fit, professional and well up to the job, I could not help noticing that my enthusiasm was not running at quite the same speed as that of my younger colleagues. To some of them it was still new and fresh; to me it was simply more of the same, and however much I enjoyed it, I could not disguise from myself that it was all becoming just a bit 'old hat'. You can only do something for the first time the once – I was just beginning to realise that. However, that thought was soon overtaken by the reality of the situation as I walked back across the Marham apron to 55 Squadron again and a reunion with a healthy selection of chums that I had flown with on occasions in the past.

It became all rather exhilarating again and I was looking forward once more to Squadron life. Needless to say, my secondary duties were led by taking back the organisation of the Station Hockey Club. My first two sorties with 55 Squadron were routine enough and I started to feel that I was settling back in harness. I then took some leave so that Maryse and I could get married.

In November, when I returned, I completed a few routine trips totalling just over eighteen hours, but by the end of the month I was assigned to the Pope crew for a week in the Mediterranean sunshine back at my old stamping ground at Akrotiri – great fun. I flew two more trips in December and then headed off home for my first Christmas with Maryse. My log book was showing just short of 3,500 hours and I was already making entries on the last available page. Log book three would arrive shortly into the New Year.

At the beginning of 1980 I took my usual skiing trip to Scotland, staying in the converted church on the Balmoral Estate; it was a boys' only expedition. The previous year, while we were still courting, Maryse had come with me and we established that skiing was not really to her liking. After the heavy rain on day three had put paid to any further fun on the slopes, I then discovered that she was really into walking, a pastime that I, too, found most agreeable and one that has stayed with us to the present day. Certainly, in recent years I have often been known to combine a good walk with a round or two of golf; although in all honesty, the more purist form of walking is still something I enjoy immensely.

Mid-February, when he returned from leave, Tony was thrown back straight into the mainstream of tanker operations. A TANSOR operation on Thursday 18 February was followed by a TACEVAL flight on the 23rd and two more on the 24th, with a maritime operation on the 26th. There had also been two 'normal' operations on the 17th, and more on the 22nd and the 25th. There was certainly no honeymoon period as far as 55 Squadron was concerned. March was equally busy with an overnight stopover at Palermo (actually Punta Raisi Airport or Falcone-Borsellino Airport as it is now known) and a couple of short night currency checks for two of the pilots.

The standard racetrack pattern for the tankers when operating out of Palermo. Refuelling was always over the sea, and wherever possible over international waters.

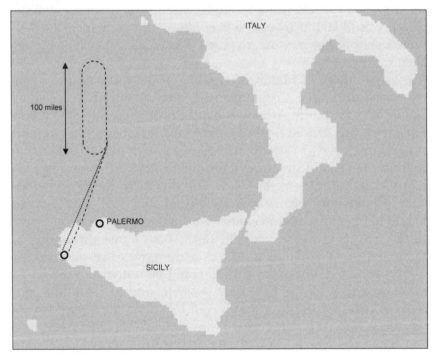

By now the situation in the Falkland Islands, South Georgia and the South Atlantic was commanding much of the headlines in the newspapers, a lot of the chatter in pub bars, and the full attention of the politicians in the Cabinet at 10 Downing Street. On 19 March a team of scrap metal merchants had raised the Argentinean flag over South Georgia and every TV news bulletin started with the story. In the Crew Room at RAF Marham the general word was that it would almost certainly come to nothing, as similar incursion episodes had in the past, but if it did come to anything it would mainly be a Navy problem to sort out. Even if the RAF were involved, then the tanker fleet would certainly not. After all there were still TANSOR flights to support and all the regular fighter training sorties to fly with only a smallish fleet of tankers to do it. It did not help the situation that a number of the Victors always seemed to be in the hands of the ground crews, having some parts replaced, repaired or refurbished. By the second week in April, despite the invasion and the surrender of the Falklands administration, the smart money around the station was still saying that the diplomacy of the USA, through General Haig, would save the day. It would all fizzle out and everyone could go home – the RAF would simply not become involved. Never had the smart money been more wrong.

By week three of March, 55 Squadron had received the signal that the code name Corporate had been allocated to cover all activities in the South Atlantic theatre. Shortly after that the whole Squadron was tasked with devising and practising the support programme needed to ferry aircraft of all sizes and speeds down to Ascension Island, and from there onward to the Falkland Islands a further 4,000 miles to the south. Still no one in the 55 Squadron Crew Room was particularly convinced that RAF involvement would happen; the station chatter was maintaining that they were simply covering the ground 'in case'. Tony's last three trips of the month on 23, 29 and 30 March were more of several needed to prove the concept that a Vulcan could be refuelled in a way to make an attack on the Falklands possible, and to create the procedures required to prove that it could be done. By 1 May Tony's Squadron had completed their many practice refuelling runs, up and down the North Sea with the ageing Vulcans and Operation

'Black Buck' had surprised the Argentineans, the Falkland Islanders and the world's press by bombing the Port Stanley airfield's only runway. The RAF was now definitely involved. Although the RAF was utilising the greater majority of its tanker fleet, Tony was still not among those heading south from Ascension on that day. He had other important things to occupy his mind.

By the last week of April we had most of the procedures for the Vulcan refuelling sorted, despite one or two moments of high drama as things went awry with the equipment and/or our getting used to flying two of the heaviest aircraft in the RAF's inventory so close together. It didn't help the programme's early days when on our first trial flight the drogue seal failed and the ensuing spray of fuel vapour quenched both pairs of engines on the receiver Vulcan. The Vulcan transmitted a Mayday and with its nose down in a pretty steep descent (to give it both the correct flying speed and to ram enough air through the turbines to facilitate an air-start), headed back to the Lincolnshire coast. We stayed with them as they glided silently through the sky and slowly, one by one, brought their engines back on line, though it was well below 10,000 feet before the first one spooled up.

Engines two and three followed soon after and height was regained for the last miles home. Once they were at altitude and out of danger, we turned and headed back to Marham. That was a close one. After remarkably few practice sorties, we became aware that our regular runs up and down the North Sea were paying off, and the feasibility of the idea was confirmed. All it needed was for detailed procedures to be written down and more practice provided for the Vulcan crews.

On 1 May we (the Peter Elliott crew) headed to RAF Boscombe Down, to the Empire Test Flying School, to chat to the boys there to start sorting the numbers for the major part of the project we had been allocated, that of tanking the RAF Lockheed C130 Hercules freighters down to the Falklands and back. The fact that this would only occur after the war was over was never up for discussion; we already knew we were going to win. To us that went without saying. What we needed was all the help we could get in order to plan the delicate operation of mating a Victor tanker that easily travelled in excess of 600 mph with a Hercules that could usually only reach just over 300 mph with the throttle levers fully firewalled. It would be an interesting hook-up to say the least, particularly as it needed to be a procedure that the newest and least experienced Victor pilot and the newest and least experienced C130 pilot could take in their stride in the midst of a tiring ten- to twelve-hour flight. That certainly gave us all something focusing to chat about over the next few days. Many cups of coffee were either drunk or allowed to go cold as the plans were formulated, redrawn and chewed over, again and again.

It was going to be a long month; my log book would show eighteen flights covering a total of over sixty-six hours before 1 June, then it would get worse as we got really busy! I flew eleven Corporate-related flights that month, spread between 1st and the 29th, with the seven other flights interspersed between them covering routine refuelling sorties. Eight of the Corporate operations were either night flights or incorporated some night flying. Not surprisingly, I did not get to see much of Maryse that summer. Oh, and I was also allocated the job of Squadron Historian as another secondary duty, just for the fun of it. There were times when the RAF really excelled itself. With this particular additional duty I really began to feel that I had really reached the status of Squadron Elder Statesman.

Next we shifted to the Nimrod trials, which by comparison, were a walk in the park and caused us no problems whatsoever. For us, it went absolutely perfectly on the first run (although we accepted that at that stage both planes were being flown by the top men from each Squadron). Nonetheless, it was heartening to have it work out right first time. We completed the second run for that operation as a night trial with equal success before heading across to our main 'problem child' within the RAF fleet, the prop-driven C130 Hercules.

What we were doing with all these tests was in reality adding new sections to the Flight Ops Manual. We had to work out all the parameters that were comfortable for the receiving aircraft: heights, speeds and positions; the optimum, minimum and maximum in all cases and also what patterns were needed to complete a full fuel transfer. We then had to establish whether it had to be flown manually or if it could be completed on auto-pilot and also how much effect the weather and air conditions would have on all phases of the refuelling sequence, from sighting to final breakaway. It was a big task.

There was a lot of work required, mental and physical, just to make sure it was possible. Then towards the end of the trials, having sorted the straight-line section for successful fuel transfer, they had to find out if the heavies could continue with the hook-up whilst in the turns of the racetrack pattern being flown by the tankers. They knew that the fighter boys could, at least when they had a bit of experience and expertise under their belts. But could the pilots of the heavies do the same with forty tons of hardware under the control column? Then of course, as mentioned earlier, there was the dear old prop-driven Hercules itself to get to grips with. This would surely stretch them all to the limit?

The most obvious problem was the speed differential mentioned earlier, however the second and equally significant problem was the fact that the practical service ceiling of the Hercules was in the low 20,000 feet area. The Victor fleet were used to operating their refuelling procedures at 30,000 feet or more and yet the C130 would be struggling to get much above 20,000 feet, let alone be controllable enough to perform the refuelling hook-up manoeuvre. There was an obvious height disparity between the two and it was of significant proportions. Much head scratching followed the visit to the civilian engineers at Boscombe Down and no doubt many further phone discussions as the first draft of the new operational plan was worked out.

The Hercules pilots had briefed their engineers before the Boscombe meeting, and our pilots then had to make sure that what everyone had agreed could actually be achieved. This time I inherited the easy bit of the problem, as all I had to do was to make sure we all arrived in the same piece of sky at the same time to complete the procedure. If ever you needed evidence that air to air refuelling was a team game involving every player in the team, then this was it.

As history shows, the real Falklands War had started on the same day we visited Boscombe Down. It was soon obvious that the initial Crew Room chatter at Marham that it was going to be the Navy's party was particularly wide of the mark.

Sure, the Navy had sent a Task Force of some fifty vessels, including several submarines and a sizable contingent of the British Press, to cover the event. But it was now becoming obvious that there was a developing role for us in the proceedings. As predicted, at about the time we finally got to grips with the C130 refuelling, the actual shooting war was over. That did not take the pressure off or make the job any easier or any less important. We were under no illusions how important it was to the top brass, as we were starting to fly both on Saturdays and Sundays on a regular basis in order to get the job completed as soon as possible.

We had planned to use a similar racetrack pattern for refuelling the heavies to the one we used when we were working with the smaller, more agile fighters, but with the major difference that this time we would be operating at 20,000 feet and 280 knots. Taking into account that the Hercules was operating at its limits in speed and altitude, we eventually had to devise a suitable dive angle so that with us throttled back, flying as slow as possible, and with the Hercules flying at full throttle in a dive, the two speeds could match and the conditions be optimised so that the refuelling could take place. However, that is jumping the gun somewhat, as we did not know that when we started the trials.

The first, 'pre-dive procedure', attempt did not go at all as planned. We arrived at the RV [rendezvous point] on time and we joined the racetrack pattern at the correct height and speed ... so far so good. Right on cue the Hercules C130 called up on the R/T. He too was on time and in position and all seemed ready to go. After all, hadn't the Nimrod trials all gone as smoothly as we had hoped, or better, so why not the C130 trials? Wrong!

We set our heading and speed. The planes connected and the HDU lights on the panel started to sequence, from red (Off) to amber (Connect) to green (Fuel Flowing). The refuelling process was now underway. After a couple of minutes the Nav/Radar came on the radio telling us all, but mainly the skipper, that the C130 was not looking at all stable or comfortable with the situation. I seem to recall the word 'wallowing' came into the conversation frequently. It simply was not working. It became obvious from the interchange between aircraft that the C130 would have to be in a dive to get the speed and handling conditions to match. We were then into plan B.

Initially, the speed and angle chosen was for us a shallow, comfortable descent that would take us about eight to nine minutes to reach both our 'pull-off' height of 4,000 feet and to complete the refuelling procedure. For the Hercules crew it appeared that it would be full throttle and nose down with everything shaking and buffeting. Even without the refuelling process, I'm sure sitting in turbulence from the wake of a heavy four-engine jet was never going to be an easy ride.

On the first try it became obvious that despite being flat out, the receiver plane was still pretty unstable and needed more speed to compensate. There was only one thing for it, we began to think that we needed a steeper dive angle to increase the C130's airspeed. The altimeters started to unwind down – past 15,000 feet, past 10,000 feet and then some seven minutes or more into the descent past 5,000 feet. All the time the Nav/Radar's comments hadn't changed, the Hercules was still looking far more unstable than anything we had refuelled before. Not only that, the refuelling process was still very slow.

At 4,000 feet, with refuelling incomplete, we called a halt to the run. The Hercules disconnected and we both climbed back to 20,000 feet again to reassess the situation and have another shot at it, hoping that we would have completed the operation before we descended to 4,000 on the second dive. Four minutes later, somewhere between 12,000 and 10,000 feet, the Hercules eased back on its throttles, the Nav /Radar glanced across and put up his thumb, the green HDU panel light went out and the red light glowed steadily to indicate that the refuelling had at long last been completed. There were sighs of relief all round, but a very real awareness that there was still a lot of fine-tuning to be done to the procedure, and quickly.

By the next day, the critical descent angles and speeds had all been re-calculated and we tried it again (500 feet per minute). This time it worked 100 per cent and the C130 was topped up well before the bottom of the first planned descent. The Nav/Radar was also able to report that the receiver plane seemed to be having a much easier time of it. I fed my data to Peter, who as my pilot and 'manager' of the trials, then coordinated all our responses and information into a refuelling addition to the Hercules and Victor's Flight Ops Manuals. These were immediately sent to the MoD for approval and to be rapidly printed up, ready to be delivered to all tanker and C130 crews for immediate implementation.

What had actually happened was not complicated to understand, perhaps a little difficult to have foreseen and fortunately very simple to correct. Once the hook-up occurred, the fuel started flowing and the weight and balance of the Hercules started to change, for the worse. After the slope and speed was corrected on the later run, the crew in the receiver plane could cater for these changes as they happened and the aircraft became far more stable and manoeuvrable. For obvious reasons, this revised descending section of the refuelling procedure, from this trial onwards, was always precipitated by the command 'toboggan'. From that point on all went well, even if some of the first C130 crews on the programme were probably still reading the revised manual for the first time as they thundered down the runway on take-off. There was no time to waste and everyone was painfully aware of the urgency of the situation.

We then settled into a steady routine of bringing all the RAF C130 crews up to speed on the new technique. We used the same racetrack pattern as we had for the first trials, except that we always climbed back to 30,000 feet on the return leg to Marham. The R/T chatter with the Hercules pilot usually gave us a good indication if all was well. If there was some doubt or he expressed some concerns, the conversation usually finished with 'talk to you back at base'. To my knowledge that usually sorted out matters and I don't recall anyone needing a second sortie.

I was pleased about that. My log book entries, and those of the rest of the Elliott crew, for May, had been sixty-six hours and those for June just over seventy-two. We were pretty shattered. Fortunately, we only ever managed one Hercules at a time – that was tiring enough. On an almost daily basis, it took almost until the end of June to train and check out everyone. However, by the time the last week of the month had arrived, so had the Elliott crew's orders to proceed to Ascension and join in the Corporate operation in place ferrying the C130s down to the Falklands. We were off to practise what we had been preaching!

The Elliott crew headed south on 26 June and took XL232 to join the tanker fleet based at Wideawake Airfield. It was an eight and a half hour trip nonstop, over water; followed by an arrival in a world that was unlike any other that they had ever experienced.

As the guide book told them, Ascension Island is a thirty-four square mile volcanic outcrop that in reality rises over 10,000 feet from the ocean floor, even though only 2,817 feet of it protrudes above the waters of the South Atlantic Ocean. When they landed, the Elliott crew were at seventeen degrees fifty-five minutes south and fourteen degrees fifteen minutes west. What this actually meant was that Africa was 900 miles away and South America just over 1,000 miles, and the Falkland Islands were a little over 3,900 miles to the south.

It was a fairly bleak and desolate place; that is, apart from the dozens of aircraft, thousands of RAF airmen, USAF personnel and civilian support staff and of course the twenty-four hour a day background noise and aircraft movement of a front-line RAF airfield working flat out. They later found out that up on Green Mountain, or in some of the more remote coves, round the island, some semblance of Ascension's former solitude could still be found. Initially, the Victor tanker crews did not have much spare time available for many sightseeing excursions. The Elliott crew's work schedule was typical, as they found when they landed. They had arrived late on the Saturday, and by early Tuesday would be on one of the primary refuelling Victors, ferrying a C130 south to complete its 8,000-mile journey between England and Port Stanley Airfield. There was no real acclimatising period for anyone.

Because the flight was simply south all the way, there were no jet lag problems when anyone arrived, it was normally just a case of tiredness from a long working day. Wideawake Airfield was aptly named. With its noisy, twenty-four hour a day, seven days a week activity creating a backdrop of noise that rarely diminished, going to sleep, even when you were totally shattered, was always going to be a major concern. When we arrived we were allocated a billet in a large static mobile home, complete with an air-conditioning system that was powered by an ex de Havilland Venom gas turbine engine located nearby. That little jet was great for the control of temperature but several points north of lousy for the noise level it kicked out.

We decided to be creative with our billet and divided it into two sections with some blankets. By sacrificing some of the space in the bed section we were able to create a very usable lounge area where we

*could sit and read and write or play cards in those rare off-duty
hours. As our Ops Centre was housed in a tent, we felt we hadn't
done too bad on the accommodation front. Also on our 'not bad'
list was the food. As well as the main USAF Mess, there were
numerous burger joints scattered round the place and one of them at
least was always open, whatever the hour. When you think there
were close to 4,000 bodies to feed on a daily basis, that was a huge
undertaking, and it worked well.*

*As well as the Ops Centre being under canvas, so were the hygiene
facilities. Both loos and showers were housed in tents and were
adequate, if not exactly the Ritz. I have to say, one of the other US-
maintained systems at Wideawake, the desalination plant so vital to
the function of these ablution facilities, was superb and supplied a
constant supply of water for the whole airfield. All the time I was
there, I never recall it missing a beat.*

*Earlier, I had thought that the months of May and June were
pretty busy, flying wise. Little did I know when I set out in XL192
on the first of the month, that July's log book figures would almost
match the combined totals of the two previous months. Having said
that, I should have soon been able to guess that when I noted ten
hours, thirty minutes for the one sortie. It was the same for everyone,
aircrew and ground crew alike, no one had a free ride.*

Refuelling flights always started in the mornings, with two
tankers designated for each operation. The primary aircraft and a
secondary aircraft were both fuelled up and ready to go at the start
of the operation. Both crews were briefed and prepared for the
sortie and all crewmembers manned the aircraft and completed
their pre-flight checks and engine start routine, through to having
all four engines running at static idle. The primary Victor would
then launch off south and head towards its *rendezvous* point. The
secondary aircraft would stay at the holding point until the primary
aircraft had reached the top of its climb (usually twelve to fifteen
minutes after take-off), had set course and confirmed that its HDU
system was fully functioning at altitude. (A ground function test
was not sufficient.)

Amongst the crews, there was a fairly standard joke in the radio
call confirming HDU serviceability. There was a bit of a competition

between the crews to see who could leave the biggest pause between 'is' and 'serviceable' in the standard top of climb call. 'Confirm HDU is ... [long pause] ... serviceable.'

The crew of the secondary tanker would then let out a collective sigh of relief and request permission from the tower to taxi the plane to its stand and shut down. This crew could then usually look forward to having the rest of the day to themselves. The ground crew would have been listening in on the radio calls and would be ready to meet them at the hardstand. Paperwork, including Form 700, would be exchanged as the aircraft was handed back to its true owners, the ground crew, and the flight crew would then head off to start their revised day.

Mostly the days started at about 5 am, when the temperature was already pleasant and warm and the breeze was gently blowing, sufficient to keep it at a comfortable level. I had two ways of starting this 'bonus' day after returning to the stand in the reserve tanker. I sometimes went straight to the beach for a couple of hours and then returned to the billet for a shower, change and a gentle amble over to the American Mess for late breakfast, brunch or lunch, depending on the time. The other routine was a variation on a theme. I would head straight for a shower, wash my flying suit (which I knew would be dry within the hour), visit the Mess for a meal ... then wander down to the beach. Either way, it was a very relaxing way to pass the time.

On known 'stand down days', we would be more adventurous and head further out and see the sights of the island. Surprisingly, despite its size and the fact that it was volcanic, I found that there were many interesting places to visit and a lot to see, certainly for someone on a fairly short stay. Although it is probably fair to say that a longer visit could well have produced a different assessment of the island's tourist attractions.

Getting away from the noise was a delight on the days off. OK, you could never get totally away from the sound of the aircraft as they took off, but a few miles away from the airfield brought a blessed relief from the drone and hum of the background noise that was always present. We played sports a great deal and frequently went walking. The Mess produced some very acceptable packed lunches when we took to the hills and plains of the interior.

Many years earlier someone had put a series of walker's posts round the island, all equipped with marker stamps; so that on the way round, you could stamp your guide map with a permanent record every time you visited one of these posts. I completed them all before I left the island for the last time. Some super fit, superheroes did them all in one day, which although I never calculated it, seemed to me to be a thirty-five to forty-kilometre round trip. Even if my guess was inaccurate and over optimistic, it still seemed a bit too much for a one-day foot sortie to me. I took it in gentle manageable stages – after all, I was one of the Squadron's Elder Statesmen, wasn't I? I could afford to leave all the athletic stuff to the younger set!

The other thing I could have happily left to the younger set was the loos. I never really ever got used to a toilet facility that had its outer walls and cubicle dividers made from thin pieces of khaki canvas that flapped happily in the breeze. It was all just one step too close to 'alfresco' for my taste. Whenever possible, I would prefer to take the walk to the Mess and use the more traditional toilet facilities that had rigid walls, ceilings and floors and were to all intents and purposes a permanent structure. On one occasion I even ducked into the station CO's en-suite facility and luxuriated for a while in a quiet, civilised and wholly acceptable set of surroundings for that part of my daily ablutions. Naturally, I had made strenuous enquiries to ensure that he was not around before I helped myself to his exclusive, top-of-the-range toilet.

On our days off we would sometimes head to the USAF PX (supermarket equivalent to the old British NAAFI) and spend an hour or so browsing at stacks of things we didn't want, or could not afford. A cheap tee-shirt could take a full hour to choose if you worked at it, especially if one or two of your crew were with you to assist with the purchase. There were open-air cinemas that had a change of programme every two or three days and there was the Mess where you could buy a drink. Somehow, no one seemed to find that as interesting as the Mess back home at Marham, and it was not as popular as one would have expected. Certainly, I cannot recall anyone over indulging on that front, mainly because you were always aware that it was not a normal situation and you could be called to fly the following day.

The Jet A1 came from a large fuel tanker anchored permanently out in the bay. One of the excursions on offer to the men stationed on the island, which was a bit different to the norm, was to take one of the organised trips out to the tanker, where a conducted tour and a BBQ would be organised. The tanker crews were on a six-month tour, as were many of the ground and admin boys – any longer would have been a bit mind bending. As such, the tanker team was always pleased to see the shore party arrive and always put on a good show for their visitors.

Mail, both in and out of the island, was via the free BFPO (British Forces Post Office) system and it worked extremely well. Occasionally, there would be a one- or two-day hiccup, and in those circumstances it was not unknown for chaps to get four or five letters in one hit. All they had to do then was to check the postmark and open them in the right order.

Despite all this, RAF disciplines and systems were still in place, daily reports still had to be written up, usually from Squadron records and aircraft logs; crews still had to stay current with their medical, flying and operational requirements, just the same as if they were back at Marham. Tony had at least one A4 report to complete each day. For the Elliott crew this pattern of life ran for the full month of July. They did nineteen sorties that month and were airborne for 132 hours, including two mammoth ten hours and forty-five minutes operations in the early part of the month. It had been a long and exhausting month when they clambered aboard XL162 on 2 August and headed north and home.

After a week's leave, they took XL189 across to St Athens for heavy maintenance and returned later the same day to Marham with its replacement. Just one night exercise followed on 24 August and then it was off back to Ascension. Home life for everyone in the tanker squadron at that time was somewhat fleeting.

This time we split our south bound flight with a short stopover in Dakar. I recall that Dakar Airport was all that I expected it to be. It was hot, dusty and for a quick refuelling halt, pretty uninteresting, despite being on a spectacular peninsula jutting out into the South Atlantic. The pilots commented that the beaches to the north of the airport looked both huge and inviting, but we would not be there long enough for even the briefest of visits. I did not know it at the time, but I would return a few weeks later and have a few hours more there to get the feel of that part of West Africa. Those extra few hours did not significantly change any of my views on the place. Two days later on the 28th we were back in the long-distance refuelling routine again and on the 30th I collected my all time record – a full eleven-hour sortie in XL158. Boy did I sleep well that night, even the drone of all the background noise, including our own air-conditioning jet unit, failed to keep me awake. The moment my head hit the pillow I was gone. Fortunately for the Elliott crew, all but two of the September operations that we were allocated were in the three- to four-hour bracket.

We were then informed that we were heading back to Marham to work on the planning of the Mansion House Victory Celebration Fly-past. Naturally, I had been allocated the navigational side of the plan to sort out. That would certainly keep me busy for a day or two and concentrate the mind more than enough. With that size and calibre of audience over central London and the theoretical size of the worldwide television audience, even the smallest blip in the accuracy of the formation would stand out. No one in the team could even begin to contemplate the possibility of such a blip, as the fall out would have been catastrophic. It had to go 100 per cent right and that was the end of the matter.

Life was never boring.

CHAPTER 12

The Victory Fly-past and Beyond

T he date chosen by the Whitehall mandarins for the celebratory fly-past over London to mark the end of the Falklands War and to publicly celebrate the victory of the British armed forces was 12 October 1982. That gave the organising teams about three weeks to plan, check, test and practise the whole programme. For Tony it represented several intense days surrounded by maps, speed data and all the other information he would need to produce a working flight plan. All he had to do was calculate a navigational plan and timetable that ensured all the aircraft involved would stream overhead the Mansion House in the City of London on time, so that the scripted TV commentary could slip seamlessly from whatever they were talking about, to the fly-past, without anyone having to look skywards to double check that it had arrived. Well that was what he was told, although he did privately harbour the sneaking suspicion that the noise that over one hundred jet engines in such a confined space would produce, might just give the game away. He kept that comment to himself. His under-standing was that Whitehall mandarins were not known for their sense of humour.

OK, so we all knew that flying east to west, keeping the Thames fairly close to our port wing, would get us more or less there, but it was a bit more involved than that. I had fast jets (well very fast jets to be brutally honest) and heavy jets at one end of the scale to coordinate with relatively slow helicopters at the other.

The speed differential was in hundreds of miles an hour – far, far more than the differential we had to deal with with the Victor/C130 refuelling situation and we had the eyes of the world upon us, with no rehearsal time planned. The first and only run through would be the real thing. Great! As they say – no pressure!

There were twenty or so attendees at each of the meetings called to organise the fly-past. Fortunately for my convenience the meetings were all held at Marham. Fortunately for the other attendees who had to travel, there were only three or four of them! By 29 September I had a draft plan sorted for the navigation and timing, and the Elliott crew did a two-hour fifty-minute proving run to make sure I hadn't missed anything. In some ways it was not as difficult as it first appeared. The bulk of the aircraft, the heavies (Victors, Vulcans, Nimrods, VC10s and C130s), all had similar speed capabilities, as did the fast, light, fighter jets that were to join us. Thus it was going to be possible for them all to maintain the required run-in speed with most of them at the lower end of their capabilities. The slower aircraft, the helicopters, would not be able to maintain anything like this sort of speed for any length of time, so they would join us at the last minute on the run-in. If they were a minute or so behind the main block when we reached Mansion House, then so be it. It would not look odd and would not cause any difficulties to them or the main body of the fly-past.

One of the thoughts most prominent in the minds of all the crews involved was that they required a full set of serviceable aircraft. Sure there was no problem if the HDU was not fully functioning on one of the Victors, or the bomb aiming kit on the Vulcan was on the blink, but all aircraft needed to be totally serviceable in all other respects. It was not that easy for anyone to take that serviceability for granted when most of the aircraft in the fly-past fleet were veterans of the war itself and had been worked exceptionally hard over the preceding months. There were 'spares' lined up for almost every position in the fly-past and they would stay with the main fleet well into the formation period of the build-up. The basic plan was that the fleet would assemble off the North Norfolk coast then turn inland and descend from its original assembly height of 20,000 feet down to its initial fly-past height of 1,000 feet as it flew over Marham and streamed south across rural Norfolk, Suffolk and Essex, heading towards the nominated holding and correction area just off the coast in the Thames Estuary.

My flight plan relied heavily on the TACANs at Coltishall and Lakenheath to provide the navigational grid for me to accurately plot and fine-tune the progress of the fleet as it headed towards London. I had planned holding patterns over Canvey Island that could hold us for quite a while if weather or any unforeseen hazard gave us a delay. It also involved a part of a standard Towline refuelling pattern that could shave off anything from a minute to a full five minutes as a correction if necessary. In the event, no such adjustment was necessary and we arrived just three seconds adrift. Timing was important, but it was not that much of a critical headache to me and the rest of the team, after all this is what we tanker crews did all day and every day as our role in the RAF. The radio calls as the formation progressed would confirm that the rest of the fleet were all doing what they should at the correct height, speed and location. My understanding of the plan was simple. The hierarchy at High Wycombe had decided what would happen, I had calculated where and at what time and what speed we needed to achieve that and we had thirty or forty of the very best pilots in the world sitting behind us to make sure that it all went according to the script. On paper it was foolproof.

Approaching the capital from the east along the Thames we were talking to the Civilian Air Traffic System and it was obvious that they had come up trumps and isolated the airways for us. The sky over London was ours. I asked Peter to ease back a touch to make the last fine correction to our arrival time. Along this leg of the flight plan, just as we reached the suburbs, the lead Victor swept across in front of us and we took over the role as number two in the formation, flanked by the pair of Harriers that we had collected earlier. We had passed on the final read-out of our time, height and speed to the helicopter boys who then pulled in behind us and followed us across

the City. Our final call to London Air Traffic Control, 'On time ...
We're coming in', coincided with the lead Victor taking up his
position. At the same time I recall becoming very conscious that not
only were the senior layers of the RAF at the Mansion House standing beside the country's leaders, but via live TV and satellite links,
the eyes of the whole world were on us as we swept over the centre of
London. It was rather like a TACEVAL. No one was going to make
their careers on this, but an obvious mess up would not do any of us
any good, that was for sure.

Six minutes later it was all over and we were all given clearance
by London Air Traffic Control to resume our own navigation and
head for home. Peter came over the radio, 'Look out the window.'
XL192 raised its nose and banked over in time for Buckingham
Palace to slip past the window some 1,500 feet below us. I know we
had been told that we were not to buzz the Palace, but the temptation
was just too strong, and besides, no one much was watching us. Even
if they were, it was doubtful if they would say anything – and sure
as heck, we wouldn't.

We completed the flight back to Marham in about twenty
minutes, just in time for the end of the official champagne reception.
The last of the bubbles had gone flat and the buffet had been reduced
to crumbs, so there was nothing left for us to do but to change
out of our kit and go home. It had been a Number One uniforms and
posh frocks sort of 'do' in the Mess, and in reality no one wanted a
couple of sweaty aircrews in overalls hob-nobbing with the Air Vice-
Marshal and his buddies. It would not have mixed too well with
the foreign dignitaries and their ladies, and the assembled crowd of the
great and the good. All things considered, it was all a bit of an anti-
climax. At the Monday morning briefing both Victor crews got a
cursory 'well done chaps' before the Wing Commander moved on to
more important matters. To the RAF, the fly-past was now history
and merely the subject matter of enthusiasts' video tapes, and a few
column inches or maybe even a short article in the aviation press.

I know they appreciated us really ...

I had a brief one-day weekend followed by a two-hour flight
the following Monday. Oh, and I also received the message that the
Squadron History Reports covering the Falkland operation thus far,
were due in by the end of November, and could I get a shift on! I

completed them on time and they duly went onward and upward for approval. When they returned some time later, I could not help but notice that not an additional 'i' had been dotted nor an additional 't' crossed. I wondered if anyone had even bothered to look at them, let alone read them and check for accuracy. Perhaps the top brass at High Wycombe were still running the videos of the fly-past? I think maybe I was getting just a tiny bit cynical.

For Tony the next two months were very much back to normal with trips back to Palermo, Ascension and one overnight and one refuelling stop at Dakar. The first Marham–Dakar–Marham trip was on 1, 2 and 3 November, with an interesting diversion on the way home for an overnight stop at Leuchars due to bad weather at Marham. The next day it was down to Palermo with a single refuelling sortie on 8 November and the flight back to Marham on the 9th. The rest of that month and December were assigned to working on Squadron History duties. Then there was just one short night training sortie on 21 December as a precursor to a rather inconvenient Christmas operation. With the Millikin crew, he took Victor XL190 down to Ascension on 23 December, completed a five-hour sortie in XL161 on the 24th and on the 25th spent the best part of Christmas day transiting XL188 back to Marham via Dakar.

That was a full nine hours forty airborne. Add to that the pre-flight preparation time on Ascension, the stopover time at Dakar and the post flight paperwork at Marham, and you can see it was a very, very long day. I returned home just as Christmas Dinner was being served. I fell asleep at the table long before we ever got to the Christmas pudding and mince pies.

Over the Christmas break, or what was left of it, I had a quick glance through my log book. My total time flown was just over 3,954 hours. The magic 4,000-hour entry would not be that far away. Sometime in the spring of 1983 I would hit that number and my guess was that my flying career would be starting to wind down and draw to a close. Anno Domini was catching up fast. In the history of the RAF, no one had ever gone straight from operational aircrew to OAP with a bus pass in one jump, and I was sure I would not be the first.

In January, for once, the gods of RAF planning smiled at Tony and he only had three short trips with a combined total of eight hours fifty-five minutes; it was a chance for his batteries to get topped up and recharged, and some sort of equilibrium to return to his life. The only trip south in February was to recover XL190, which he had taken down to Ascension on the Christmas special as part of the Millikin crew. The rest of the month was not over-taxing either, and included being loaned out to 232 OCU for a training sortie on 18 January.

No good deed goes unpunished as they say, so on 3 March I joined the Russell crew and headed back south, again dog-legging into Dakar on the way down to Ascension, as had become almost standard practice. The usual one day's rest followed and we were back in business on 5 March. That was a ten-hour trip, but fortunately it was the longest by far during the whole month. It was on a shortish flight a few days later, on 14 March 1983, that the 4,000 hours landmark was reached and I landed back at Wideawake on 4,001 hours and 54 minutes' total time airborne. I had also reached that other notable landmark with a four in it that is significant in any flyer's life. I was now forty years old, flying with chaps almost young enough to be my sons. The early mornings seemed earlier, the long flights seemed longer and the novelty of slumming it in a trailer park serviced by loos with flappy canvas walls, had long since lost its appeal. I know I was one of 55 Squadron's Elder Statesmen, and I was really starting to warm to the status and the comforts and dignity I hoped it would bring. Sadly by the spring of 1983 those perks of age and seniority had not yet reached as far south as Wideawake Airfield.

April saw Tony back at Marham for a short while. On 6 April he was practising for an Open Day fly-past that occurred for real just two days later on Friday 8 April. May was equally as quiet compared with the duties at Ascension, though he did have a mixed bag of pilots to fly with, including several Flight Lieutenants (Russell, Wood, Jones and Brooks), a Squadron Leader (Tiernan), a Wing Commander (Vallance) and a USAF Captain on an exchange tour from the American Military (Boehn). The Brooks trip was another 232 OCU loan flight, as one of the new boys made his way to the tanker squadrons via Marham's hard-working conversion unit.

June was a very short month flying wise, which allowed Tony's secondary duties and other RAF Marham occupations to kick in. There was more hockey to organise and play, more Squadron history to document and the occasional need to host visitors who were on official visits to the station. Having availed himself of the squash courts and gym facilities at Wideawake and taken almost every opportunity to walk or swim during his time off on Ascension, his fitness levels had not suffered, and so he was able to slot straight back into playing matches without any problem.

July was a pretty normal sort of flying month, heralding a short August with two weeks' summer leave thrown in towards the end of the month. Needless to say, the shortened August was again an easy month with just four sorties including two TANSOR operations on the 22nd and 24th.

In October, just over two months after working with him during his OCU training, he took F/Lt Brooks out to Cyprus via Palermo, staying overnight at Akrotiri on 25 October. Once again, Tony was able to take the opportunity to enjoy a spot of horse riding with the local riding club in the warmth of the late autumn sun in the Eastern Mediterranean – good relaxation before a further short trip back to Ascension in November. December at Marham was quiet, but it was sufficient to bring Tony's log book past 4,200 hours.

As I knew I was going to Ascension for a month in February 1984, I took my skiing holiday in the January of that year. Because of this I only had two trips that month. As usual I made up for it once I arrived at Wideawake and although the number of sorties was fairly high, the hours were not so great as they were all fairly short trips. In our absence that month a TACEVAL had been planned by the NATO hierarchy, so as part of the Rees crew I flew a TACEVAL sortie on my last trip in March. April and May were pretty standard 55 Squadron tanker months for me with a fairly light load of TANSOR operations and a variety of training exercises.

By late June I knew that I was heading towards my last few months as aircrew, and although the month of June had been quiet, the RAF decided that my last flying month would be fairly busy. I flew for nearly twenty-five hours on nine sorties with six different captains and in six different aircraft on what seemed like a good representation of my entire flying RAF career.

However, as the saying goes, all good things come to an end and in the early evening of 31 July when I stepped down from Victor XM715, I knew my RAF flying days were at an end. I had flown in every continent of the world, in well over a dozen different countries and with several hundred superb pilots and fellow crewmembers. I had logged 4,326 hours of my life airborne, and I did not regret a single minute of it. I had never had to 'bang out', I had never crashed and I had only had one major engine failure that gave my pulse any reason to gallop a bit. Sure, like all aircrew, I had encountered the occasional equipment failure, like the loose oil pipe on a diminutive Army Scout and the occasional electrical glitches, but never more significant than requiring a premature return to base to get it fixed or to swap to a different aircraft. I had been extremely lucky on many counts, but it was now time to put that behind me and move on.

CHAPTER 13

Operations Again

When I hung up my flying overalls in the wardrobe for the last time that Tuesday evening, as Maryse and I prepared to head off for our summer break, I realised that from then on I would always return to work at Marham in my Number Two uniform. It would seem strange to approach Number Four hangar and then turn left to go to my new home, the Intelligence Section of the Operations bunker, rather than turn right and head towards 55 Squadron. It would be equally strange not to go flying and almost unreal to think I would not be aircrew ever again. However, that is how it was, Anno Domini had seen to that.

While I was away on leave, I was being processed through the security machine again. This was essential, for despite my background, JARIC, and all my years in the RAF, such was the sensitivity of the bunker that this was a pre-requisite for anyone going in there to work. If you were a visitor (that in itself would be a very rare situation), then you were escorted by your sponsoring officer into the specific room that you had been cleared to visit and then escorted out again after your business had been completed. Other than that, whoever you were, whatever your rank, you simply did not get in. Under escort I had earlier been allowed into the bunker to see where my room was located, but that was all until my security documents came back with all the ticks in all the appropriate boxes.

My first job in the new post would be on the receiving end of the handing over procedure for the entire portfolio of official documents, as well as the War Book, and other classified material. It took just one line in my diary to note its happening, but it would take a full four weeks looking at and signing for, each item that was within my new remit.

Before that I had to meet my team. I asked my Sergeant to bring in the coffee and to sit down. I remember I started the conversation with all of them the same way. 'What do you do?' I worked my way from the Sergeant via the Corporals to the airmen, until I had a pattern in my mind of all my team and their respective duties. Then it was a case of heads down and working our way stoically through the handover. As with all military situations, the Sergeant was the cornerstone to the smooth running of the operation; he had been in situ at Marham for just over three years and in the RAF Intelligence Section for over ten. He knew his stuff. In reality, the whole team were very much on the ball and in all the time I was there they always put in 100 per cent. I never once had to pull rank to keep them in line or get anything done. To me, we operated more like an experienced aircrew, than a loosely assembled group of office types. I had inherited a really good team.

After one month, Tony's predecessor S/Ldr Les Sweeney left Marham and was off to pastures new and F/Lt A.F. Golds was installed as Senior Intelligence Officer. Over the next three years there would be several fixed patterns within his new area of responsibility and several non-standard sorties into pastures new. On the routine side, he had a security briefing to give to the Station Commander and his senior officers on a weekly basis. Every month he gave a briefing to the squadrons on any update in the situation within the Warsaw Pact that NATO surveillance had uncovered, since the last briefing. In turn, he had to attend briefings himself at both High Wycombe and Ashford, as other relevant data and information was disseminated from High Command to the various operational bases. The non-routine assignments included going on exercises with the Army in a liaison/intelligence role, being temporary Station Commander at RAF Holbeach on three separate occasions and being part of the inspection team invigilating the MINEVALs at nearby RAF stations at Honington and Wittering.

My new abode was a pretty austere place compared with the traditional Squadron Crew Room that was my normal service home. I think it would be fair to say its design and upkeep was purely functional and bore no allegiance to any current architectural or decorative style.

The building itself was in reality an incredibly huge concrete block with rooms and corridors interwoven in its interior. These rooms and corridors were all similarly painted in a less than fetching shade of light grey and interspersed with a selection of very functional doors, some of which were wooden and others that were made of steel. None would have received a second glance in any design competition.

It was a massive structure that was hopefully designed to withstand most forms of attack, but we were under no illusion whatsoever that we were by definition a primary target for the Warsaw Pact should a real shooting war ever start. Marham was that important in the NATO operation. Once I had passed the outer fence, armed guard, and a number of checkpoints just to reach my room, beyond that, even deeper into the massive concrete monolith, there were more huge steel doors. I occasionally went through into the inner sanctum to the Operations Room, but that was as far as I wanted to go. I was more than happy just to evaluate, code and then disseminate the information, regardless of by what means it had arrived at the Marham teleprinter printout. Usually it was by spy plane or satellite.

The spy satellites were a mixed blessing. In 1984 we had a good supply of up-to-the minute information flowing through to us from our data-gathering people. Our satellites gave us a whole host of information that would have been vital should hostilities have broken out between ourselves and the Soviet Union (as it was called back then, in the cold war period). Their importance and the information they provided was paramount whether it was an all out war, or only a minor third party, border skirmish between two junior NATO and

Warsaw Pact member states. Unfortunately, the Russians were at a similar state of intelligence gathering as ourselves and we knew that they had two satellites passing directly over Marham every day, no doubt having a good 'look-see' at what we were up to. Needless to say, we always attempted to operate in a way that their spy satellite windows (six minutes) were not able to see anything of value, particularly with the nuclear side of things. Effectively, this meant nothing 'sensitive' moved anywhere on the airfield. When this satellite overfly was giving me a bad day, I earnestly hoped our NATO spy satellites were causing their intelligence people as much of a problem. That seemed a reasonable exchange to me.

The liaison work with the Army, at Keeble, which came fairly soon after taking up the new role, had shades of *déjà vu* for Tony, as it was two weeks under canvas; very similar to Ascension but with more rain and without as much heat. It also had loos with canvas walls that flapped in the breeze! Nothing changed. His titles for this exercise were Intelligence Officer and Air Force Support. It was a twenty-four hours a day, seven days a week operation and he worked what seemed to him a twenty-hour day, every day. There was just Tony and one Flying Officer to share the load. Tony hated writing up the reports; his Flying Officer took to it like the proverbial duck to water. However, giving presentations and lectures, was an area in which Tony was in his element. This meant an obviously natural split of responsibilities and it worked superbly.

However, there were a few upsides to all this. By day two, Tony had realised that while armies may well march on their stomachs, the General in charge, and his entourage, travelled and ate in a far more civilised manner. They partook of a much better menu; one that was much more to Tony's palate than the corned beef and mash that the greater mass of Army types were tucking in to, on the other side of camp. He and his younger colleague decided to attach themselves to the General's team, especially at meal times. A steak with all the trimmings was infinitely preferable to a couple of slices of corned beef and a dollop of mash, especially if there was the odd glass or two of red to wash it down. As he reasoned to his young RAF colleague at the time, 'You just

never know, the General may well have wanted to discuss something important with us over dinner.' As it happened, he never
did.

*Then there was the day when the Group Captain phoned and asked
me to pop into the office before I went home.*

*'Change of office for you next week, Tony, you're off to the
Holbeach Ranges on Monday to look after things for a couple of weeks
there. Their CO has gone on leave . . . need a fill in.' Not bad, instant
Station Commander – in one easy lesson. All I had to do was turn
up, listen to the Corporal and Warrant Officers who ran the place,
and provided I more or less left everything alone and didn't interfere,
all would be well.*

*I turned up at Marham early the following Monday and was
driven in a staff car to my new job. I made a mental note as we sped
along the A47 towards Sutton Bridge, that in future I must make
arrangements to drive myself there straight from home. I was taking
twice as long to get to work as necessary and tying up a staff car and
driver that I didn't really need. However, just for once, it was a bit
of an ego trip to travel in the manner of the Group Captain, even if I
was only his stand-in for a couple of weeks.*

*I presented my F1250 Identity Card at the gate and walked
in to my new station. At my 'proper' job I was well supervised by
the Sergeant who ran things most efficiently; the equally well run
admin section of RAF Holbeach was the domain of a Corporal, who
obviously graduated from the same training school as my Marham-
based Sergeant.*

*My Corporal greeted me as I entered the admin block. After the
initial salute and pleasantries he enquired if I would like coffee and
did I take milk and sugar and if so how many? I knew at that point
that he was right on top of things and that we would get on fine.
Apart from my Corporal, I had a team of three Warrant Officers who
ran the range itself, along with three further Corporals and four
airmen. They organised and operated all the 'hands on' part of the
operation out on the edge of the Wash and measured and recorded
the bombing accuracy of our visitors. We tended to get a combination
of two, three or four planes an hour. Two was the favourite amount,
three was acceptable, but four was felt to be pushing the boundaries*

a little and compromising the team's ability to provide the right quality of service.

There was also a contingent of RAF fire fighters on site who lived with their fire engine and other safety and rescue kit, away to one side of the complex. They were never needed while I was there on this or any of my other two tours in charge of the place. However, we were always mindful that on several occasions since the range's initial opening to the present day, the RAF had the misfortune on occasion to drop the odd plane or two into the mud of the ranges when something had gone seriously awry at low level.

The most obvious improvement I noticed when I sat at my desk for the first time was that the coffee was real – genuine, percolated, coffee-tasting, aroma-giving, real coffee. None of your hastily prepared 'RAF standard issue', instant stuff here. I suddenly felt sure I was going to enjoy the next fortnight. I was also going to enjoy the fact that not only was my Corporal a totally switched on guy, but so were the Warrant Officers down on the range itself. They had the whole station professionally buttoned up. They were 100 per cent on the ball and had the place humming like the proverbial well oiled precision machine. They certainly didn't need me to run the operation, they had that well under control. All they needed was the strength of the costume jewellery on my uniform that went with being a F/Lt; to sign forms, make phone calls and generally add the muscle of rank if it was needed. All the time I left things alone, all would be well and the station would function like clockwork.

The flying programmes into the Wash Ranges were all prepared weeks in advance, so my only real solo duties of any significance were to monitor the weather from a flying perspective. Weather conditions could open or close the ranges, or sometimes delay the start of the day's proceedings if the morning mists were slow to clear. The other job was to monitor the flying schedule lists and fill any vacant slots created if a particular squadron could not fulfil their allocation, for whatever reason. It was almost certainly a job my Corporal could have handled without blinking, but it was in the rule book that it had to be the officer in charge who made the decisions, so that one landed on my desk. Occasionally, we were advised that the bomb runs for the day would contain some pyrotechnics. On those occasions most of the team did their best to assemble at vantage points around the station to watch the private, and very expensive, firework display.

It was one of those really enjoyable periods of my RAF career that simply sped past with indecent haste. I was quite sad to leave 'my' little team when I reached the last Friday of my command. That sadness would have been softened somewhat if I had realised that I would return to RAF Holbeach twice more as temporary Acting Station Commander before I eventually left the Air Force for good.

However enjoyable it was out at the edge of the Wash, once the two weeks were up, it was back to RAF Marham, the bunker, and reality for Tony. He may well have stood in for the real CO of RAF Holbeach while he went on holiday to the sunshine of the Canaries, or trekking in the Andes, or wherever; but the holiday reality for Tony was that he had to stay in the UK and he had to stay very close to a phone all the time, and he had to be able to return to duty at very short notice. That was part of the job spec, as was letting the station CO know where he could be contacted, at all times. The main concern was the fact that there were signals that came into the station all the time that were for the CO and Tony's eyes only; there was no real number two with this job.

If Holbeach was one of the lighter areas of his duties, then one of the other duties that followed it at Marham, the annual MINEVAL, was one of the more intense. Previously he had experienced it from the flying end, now he was face to face with the operational aspects of it. Initially of course, there was the need to write and plan the MINEVAL itself. That usually started at least four weeks before the klaxons sounded on day one. At the first meeting to discuss the upcoming exercise, the Station Commander would have a few new ideas up his sleeve, as well as a resumé in his notes of the areas of weakness from the previous event. To Tony, as the operational invigilating officer for the MINEVAL, this was a set of directions he would have to incorporate in his plans so that these weaknesses could be seen to have been ironed out. After all, a full-scale NATO-run TACEVAL could follow within weeks and there should be no sign of any previously self-recognised weakness in the system.

Senior officers were acutely aware that their RAF careers would not be made on a TACEVAL, but they could easily be lost on one. Hence the importance they placed on the lessons to be learned from the 'home grown' MINEVAL. During this build-up period, junior officers were frequently made fully aware of their master's view on the subject; 100 per cent effort was the minimum required from everyone, starting with the organising team. There was also a continual stream of MoD types coming in to check that all was well in the bunker. They checked and analysed some of the more basic procedures and processes, that all paperwork was up to date, and that out-of-date papers and codes were disposed of in the correct manner. Needless to say, all normal operations had to continue at full strength while all this was going on. Tony's years spent at JARIC were paying off.

In previous postings it had never occurred to me that I needed to be careful about my off-station activities. Before this, a skiing accident whilst on holiday would have been a bit embarrassing for a couple of weeks and would have meant I had my leg pulled unmercifully for the next six months or so. With this job I had no idea what a period of total incapacity in the job would have done, or how it would have been handled. There was only one other officer who knew most of what I did, but that was it. Even my stalwart support team, including my Sergeant, did not have access to all the areas and information that went with my responsibility. For the moment I would have to be ultra careful and responsible in both my service and my private life.

The high point of every year and the reinforcing of the pivotal situation I found myself in with this job was never more focused than when we had a MINEVAL taking place. When I was in Operations on the Squadron, the MINEVAL was pressure enough; now down in the bunker it was the same, but ramped up 100 per cent. The pattern followed the same as that on the Squadron, except that instead of waiting for the scenario briefing, I was the one putting it together and delivering it. I was also the person who received the aircraft readiness status from the Squadrons and fed that into the equation and passed it on to the Station Commander as part of my briefings to him. I had to be really careful to avoid opinions (mine and others) and I had to ensure that in my report I only passed on verifiable facts, not even trends or projected data based on those known facts. The interpretation and analysis of those facts was strictly for those higher up the RAF food chain than me.

The Tannoy announcements that I had listened to so intensely during my time in Squadron Operations were now part of my remit, which I delivered from a small broadcasting desk just down the corridor from my room. I was conscious that there were people listening to my every word and timing the whole event from start to finish, as well as noting if I had actually managed to start on time. I only rarely passed this duty on to my Sergeant. He was certainly fully capable of doing the job, but most of the time he had enough to do with his own duties, as well as double-checking on me and the team. This was a job that he did most admirably, and certainly a great deal of the credit of our section's smooth running was down to him; I don't recall us ever getting it even slightly wrong.

By the end of hour one I needed to present a 'broad picture' briefing of the threat to the Station Commander. I then had five hours to get to grips with more of the detail to present the Station Commander and his team with a fuller briefing, and to then head to the Squadrons to present them each with a briefing to match their allocated tasks, all of which would have been issued to them just prior to my arrival. By then, information was literally pouring in regarding supposed enemy troop, aircraft and shipping movement from the Arctic, through the near Atlantic to the Mediterranean and all points in between. It was after this that the next Tannoy announcement would have been needed with a further 'pep-talk' on the requirement for maintaining vigilance and security across the whole base. This Tannoy broadcast would be updated and re-broadcast three or four times every day throughout the whole MINEVAL.

By the time that day one was playing out, my Sergeant would be sorting the team, trying to get some of them out of the way, to get them fed, washed and rested, and maybe even get some sleep. We were all going to be shattered by the end of day four, there was no point in burning out the whole team in the first twenty-four hours; even with some well planned, minimal breaks that burnout would occur naturally by the end of day four. That was when, according to the scenario, the full-scale, all-out nuclear war would hit us. By then, the situation was simple, either we were ready or we were not.

Back at the MINEVAL we still had to cope with over seventy-two hours of a full-on, frenetic workload. By early on day two I had a good picture of aircraft availability from the Squadrons, and could now include these numbers in the briefing I made to the Station Commander for his planning scenario. From past experience we were aware that by now there would be mini attacks on the airfield by air and possibly by 'enemy' land forces, though in our bunker we heard and saw nothing of these incursions.

Day three saw more individual briefings for Tornado aircrew. This could cover anything up to five or six individual crews, all of whom had separate roles to play and needed separate targets to be briefed, usually in their own Hardened Aircraft Shelter (HAS) sites. To get there I was allocated a vehicle, a driver and a fully 'tooled-up' armed guard. Anyone approaching me without authorisation could well have been shot! At least that was always the perceived theory. The airfield at that stage was virtually deserted, apart from the ground crew teams scurrying about preparing their aircraft, ready for a flight that could be called at literally a minute's notice. Needless to say, even while this was going on, the regular Tannoy messages needed to be broadcast to the station and briefings given to the CO. All this had to continue unabated as the scenario was unfolded for us to react to and as we needed to decode it and disseminate it to the waiting station.

By day four we were in a full-scale war mode and aircraft were dispatched throughout the day to carry the fight to the enemy and take out their most important strategic positions and facilities. Hopefully, this would be before they were able to unleash their own deadly weaponry on the UK, and do to us what we were hoping to do to them.

Day five included the wash-up meetings with my team and the obligatory report writing and analysis of the events relating to our section – if we felt we had done well or on occasions, if we could have done better. There would, of course, be a set of the official report documents presented to the Station Commander and his organising team by the invigilator team. The reports evaluated the complete station response from the first klaxon on day one through to the *moment on day five when the command team called a halt to it all. From this we would all learn what was needed to improve, refine, and even in some cases, repair, situations in order to prepare the station for the inevitable NATO-run TACEVAL.*

In many ways, to an outsider's casual glance, the TACEVAL was much the same animal as the MINEVAL; however, to those on the inside it was a million or more miles apart. Firstly, everyone knew when a MINEVAL was likely, even those not on the organising team could work it out. Then there would be the time since the last one, which was always a pretty good clue for even the lowliest of airmen on the station to work out. Also, there was the frequency of the disappearance of the CO and senior officers into meetings and huddles as they planned and checked progress towards the rapidly approaching MINEVAL zero hour. What they wanted was to make sure, as far as possible in advance, that the station would get a thorough checkout to prepare them for the excruciating thoroughness of the TACEVAL that would inevitably follow.

The build up to a TACEVAL also bore the same time-line programme. If RAF Marham had not had one within eighteen months, then it was almost a racing certainty that there was one just round the corner. It might hit in a day or two or it might take a week or more, but there was no way it would stretch past a month. In the lead up towards a MINEVAL, there would always have been the noticeable warnings to alert everyone. With a TACEVAL there was no such lead up warnings; just the shattering of the night-time peace as a telephone started ringing in your bedroom – always well after midnight and certainly long before dawn.

You know what it is like when you are awoken from a deep sleep by the telephone ringing or the doorbell chiming. Initially, as you struggle between unconsciousness and consciousness, you almost have to decide whether it is reality or if you are dreaming, then a split second later the phone rings for the second time and the dream option disappears. This was how it was, that was the reality; the voice at the other end started the one-sided conversation with 'Sir', and the advice was that there was a call out. The words were exact, precise and bore all the classic hallmarks of a man knowing that his every move was being monitored and noted. That is bad news at 3 am ... that is a TACEVAL ... no question. With that call you instinctively knew your life and that of thousands of other men at Marham and their families had just been put on hold and that it would be a very, very long day, followed by an equally long week. I always had a small overnight 'emergency' bag prepared for such situations, in which I had a couple of sets of underwear, a handful of handkerchiefs, washing and shaving kit and a spare shirt or two. I instinctively grabbed the bag as I dived through the door and out into the darkness of a Norfolk night.

Twenty minutes later as I drove up the hill towards the main gates, I entered a world of organised chaos. About four miles out I had started to hear the cacophony of the sirens and klaxons above the noise of my car engine. The glow in the sky grew in size and intensity as the station drew closer. When I drove up the hill, my vision was filled with shadowy figures silhouetted against the blaze of security lights flooding the area. Several hundred yards before the camp main gates the public road was blocked with a barricade manned by several airmen in combat uniform, fully armed with automatic rifles. Without a valid F1250 pass no one would be getting any further along this particular road tonight. As the barrier was moved to one side to allow me to drive through, the number of shadowy figures running or cycling furiously in the general direction of the airfield, multiplied alarmingly. I turned right off the public road and passed rapidly through the main gate, manned by double the usual number of guards and Military Police. For the duration, vehicular traffic was reduced to a few key personnel only, which fortunately included me – hence the large volume of foot traffic. There was no queue of cars to contend with at the main gate and I was soon at the first set of gates to my bunker. TACEVAL day one was about to start for real.

The airmen in the Intelligence Section lived on the station and were therefore already in and working by the time Tony got to his room. As he walked in the door, there was an array of envelopes laying in order on his desk. There was also the ominous presence of the NATO evaluation invigilator already standing in the corner of the room with his pen, recording Tony's arrival time and starting the full evaluation process. Throwing his 'overnight' bag into the opposite corner to his NATO 'spook', stepping behind his desk and picking up the first envelope and opening it, was all part of a single, smooth continuous movement, which culminated with him sitting down at his desk with the first signal in front of him. Apart from a few short breaks later in the proceedings, that was where he would stay for the greater majority of the next four days, complete with his NATO shadow, who changed with the need to keep the NATO contingent fed, watered and allowed sleep periods. From now on he would only eat, drink, sleep and even escape down the corridor to the loo, as and when the workload allowed. By experience he knew that it would allow nothing at all for the first hour as the overall situation was assessed and the Station Commander's first briefing was being collated. The Sergeant would have already arrived and would be tending to the teleprinter in the corner. It would be chattering almost continuously for the next four days as the 'make believe' scenario was unfolding hour by hour and minute by minute for the station to react to, and be assessed by the NATO invigilators. Tony's job at that stage was to check the incoming messages, decode them and in reality discard those not applicable to Marham Intelligence and place the applicable information received on the map pinned to the boards in the next room. All the data he required to create the full picture of the threat as it unfolded would need to finish up there. As a matter of security it was also a very definite requirement to cover the map when it was not being worked on.

Tony never spoke to the invigilator, nor did the Sergeant. The only communication was with the Corporal or one of the airmen who enquired as to whether one or two sugars were required with the tea, though that would be well into the second or third hour before that question arose. As with the MINEVAL, by hour one the first situation report to the Station Commander was required. As Tony went down the corridor between his bunker and the Operations bunker, the NATO spook followed dutifully one pace behind, taking notes as he walked.

The pace of the information coming into the Intelligence Section, and subsequently to Tony to evaluate, was astronomical. The main problem was sorting the useful data from that which could be listed 'interesting but not relevant'. There was a vast quantity of both. The incoming data covered all Warsaw Pact forces; land forces and movements including ICBM; tank and troop movement; air force build up and re-deployment; and all naval movements, both in port and on the high seas. It was the equivalent of doing a very large jigsaw with the picture moving and expanding all the time. There was simply no possibility for anyone in Tony's team to take their eye off the ball; if they had, for just one moment, not only would the spooks notice it, but the total plot could have been lost and from that point on, almost impossible to recover. Everyone therefore paid attention at all times.

The next CO's briefing would not be for another four hours, unless of course the TACEVAL planners threw a real oddball situation at them that needed a urgent update going to the Station Commander. (On one occasion at another station, one of the senior officers was coached to put on the thespian performance of his life, acting out the scenario of a key officer totally losing it under pressure and needing to be sent for urgent medical attention. He was eventually 'escorted away' under armed guard.) Fortunately for Tony's team, there was no such Oscar-winning dramas and the next few hours were spent organising the boys into two operational shifts and providing the resting shift with food and a brief period of sleep. It was a short-lived respite as they would be on duty again in about five hours. For Tony himself there would be no sleep yet, just the chance of a lukewarm cup of coffee and a thirty-second trip to the loo, if he was lucky.

I knew by now that the NATO countermeasures, Lockheed C130s, would be airborne and all the electronic-jamming procedures would be in place. It was also a racing certainty that the British Polaris submarines, armed with the UK's strategic ICBMs, would be up to full alert and that all the Tornado squadrons loaded with the inert tactical nuclear ordnance on board would be similarly gearing up in readiness.

By hour thirteen or fourteen the first crew change would have taken place and I would have ensured that the changeover had occurred as seamlessly as we had practised it during earlier rehearsals and MINEVALs, and that the team was still functioning as planned. It was also my first real opportunity to grab a very quick trip to the bathroom for a much needed freshen-up and then a few hours' sleep until the hard working teleprinter shifted up a gear at about 2 am for the start of day two.

As well as an update for the Station Commander, one of my first duties of the new day was to make a Tannoy briefing to the station as a whole to cover events thus far. There would also be the briefings for bomber squadrons to follow and maybe individual ones to some of the Tornado crews. Somehow it always seemed in these situations that the freshen-up had helped me more than the few hours' sleep I had managed to snatch. I learned during exercises and MINEVALS to always make sure I somehow found time to have a wash and shave; for me it paid dividends in terms of alertness and concentration. It was during this time in the early hours that my Sergeant grabbed his opportunity for a few hours' rest.

I always found my briefings to the senior staff relatively easy. They only wanted the facts and they always received whatever I had to tell them with unflappable calmness and confidence. As Marham attracted the best of the Officer Corps that the RAF had to offer at the time, perhaps that should not have come as much of a surprise.

Day three marked the halfway point of the TACEVAL. Tiredness was really beginning to bite at all levels. Individual briefings to the Squadrons and in some cases separate briefings to individual Tornado crews dominated Tony's day. All the aircraft were by now fully fuelled and loaded with the inert ordnance needed for their designated targets. As with the procedure for the MINEVAL, Tony's briefing to the Tornado crews took place in the Hardened Aircraft Shelters (HAS) where the planes and crews lived for the duration of the TACEVAL. Most of the Tornado crews would attend, except those sitting in their aircraft as the crews at the maximum of the full standby mode. Tony gave the overall intelligence picture; the crews by then would have their operational brief and would already have their target information in map and cassette form. Again, it was a fully armed escort trip from the bunker to the HAS and back. If it was beyond the point where a major attack was deemed as likely, then he and his escort would be in full NBC suits. This meant a series of wash-downs as he entered the HAS through the airlocks and dosimeter checks for radiation, or other contamination of any sort, at the NBC testing stations. Terrorist activity could be expected on or near the base and mock air attacks could well be thrown in by nearby RAF stations just to add to the confusion. After all, it was not meant to be a fun day!

Food had started to arrive at reasonably regular intervals and coffee, hot, warm and cold, depending on the workload, was delivered to my office in a non-ending stream. The meals were usually of the hot pies and chips, or beef stew variety. Not perhaps cordon bleu, *but nonetheless very welcome as the energy levels had started to drop as the long hours took their toll.*

By day four, we were aware that the scenario was leading us to an all-out war, so sleep when available was a priority. My Sergeant would always allow me my full four to five hours unless there was any sudden or additional crisis that I needed to be briefed on. The teleprinter in the early hours of day four went into orbit and a Nuclear War scenario unfolded. I re-briefed everyone as the drama intensified. Aircrews were issued with their side-arms and one or two aircraft were launched early in the day to probe the enemy's defences. My re-brief to the bomber crews at this stage always covered asking if they were mentally prepared and ready to eliminate thousands of human beings, men, women and children alike, by completing their assigned task. Any sign of hesitation had to be wheedled out and that crew or crewmember removed at once. I was never confronted with that situation in any of my briefings and I have to say that with the calibre of the senior officers and the quality of the aircrew at Marham, that did not surprise me in the slightest.

Day five was the shortest and usually comprised a few last-minute changes to keep us all on our toes and the launch of our strike against the enemy. We waited for the aircraft to return and when they did, the TACEVAL was over. All that was left was the post-mortem, the de-briefings, the paperwork and the tidying up.

As the last plane landed, my spook shut his notepad and literally disappeared without a word. All my classified material had to be accounted for, taken back to its permanent home, locked away in its correct file, and secured in the vault, ready for its next outing, which could of course have been the very next day. On one such occasion, one sheet of a minor yet still important document failed to return to its correct home. I knew it was safe but it took my Sergeant and I several anxious weeks to re-locate it in the correct cabinet, but in another file fairly close to where it belonged.

It was between eight and nine in the evening when I eventually arrived back home at Boughton. I headed straight to the bathroom for a bath, shave and the full leisurely use of all the other porcelain facilities it contained. By and large it would take my digestive system a full week to recover from the mauling it had just received. Unsurprisingly, sleep did not always come quickly that night, as my adrenalin levels struggled to get back to normal.

Normality for Tony, some time after the TACEVAL experience, was the usual three-year posting. He was on the move again, this time to West Raynham near Fakenham in North Norfolk, for a four-month course on the superb Bloodhound Anti-Bomber missile system. The journey time was only fifteen minutes' longer than the one to Marham, so there was no need for a move or overnight accommodation in the Mess. That was on the plus side. Also in the Bloodhound's favour was the fact that it was new and very different, and as another tour as aircrew at the age of … well … mid-to-late forties, was never going to happen again, it seemed like a reasonable proposition. Except that it wasn't. The journey to West Raynham through the glorious Norfolk countryside was pleasant enough. The theory side of the course was no problem whatsoever. On the negative side, the idea of living in a darkened underground shoe box with your own giant TV screen as company was not at all appealing and no great fun. The practical aspects of the course were a total anathema to him. To Tony the whole thing was little more than playing a big computer game. This was by no means on a par with being aircrew or in Operations and there was simply no teamwork or camaraderie whatsoever. It just did not press any of his buttons.

My associates on the course were in the main young pups in their early twenties whose idea of good fun was to spend all afternoon in a darkened amusement arcade feeding coins into slots in electronic machines and steadily increasing the wealth of the arcade owners. That was not my scene at all. My idea of a satisfactory mispent youth was evenings in the Mess with fellow aircrew and a reasonable supply of beer. Failing that a nice meal out with friends, or a formal evening or dance with like-minded chums and a generous smattering of lovely ladies to share the time and the dance floor. The idea of sitting for hours on end, staring at a machine that was forever blinking at you with a battery of randomly located lights and that kept up a barrage of inhuman noises, squeaking, burping and bonging at you like a demented child's toy with battery overload, was never on my agenda. I simply did not connect with it at all.

My final assessment on the Bloodhound course was 'Not good enough'. It was the first and only course I ever failed whilst in the RAF, and even as I was advised of the instructor's assessment I was inwardly starting to feel very relieved. I was not cut out for this sort of thing and very pleased not to be asked to get involved any further. How anyone ever imagined it could replace being aircrew, I had not the slightest idea. With that now behind me, I would be going back to Marham – I couldn't have been more delighted.

Tony was reassigned to the Victor Planning Centre, behind the main briefing room in the Operations block. There he was to take over from his old chum and the RAF 'God' of air to air refuelling, Ernie Wallis. He was back amongst friends and like-minded souls and involved with an area of RAF operations that he knew well and enjoyed enormously. He would be planning the flights and activities of RAF Marham's Tanker Fleet and he would be heavily involved in planning scenarios for the station's forthcoming MINEVALs and TACEVALs, those very same operations that had once given him so much trouble and had used all his military expertise to keep on course. His day to day liaison would be with the three squadron Planning Officers managing the operations of the tankers, prioritising the needs of the ongoing Tornado development programme out of Warton and of course looking after the ever present TANSOR requirements to monitor the Russian air and naval activities.

Whilst replacing Ernie was a near impossible task, taking over from him was always going to be easy. He had made sure of that before he vacated the office for the last time and turned it over to me. He was 100 per cent professional and it showed. All I had to do was walk in the office and sit down and start work, even the pencils in the drawer were sharpened ready to use. The next week's programme was already there, completed as far as possible, just needing the final last-minute additions that were 'hot off the presses'. I liaised with the Squadron planning boys then set to work on the following week's plan. It all fell instantly into place.

My first week in most ways set out the pattern that I would follow for the rest of my time in that section. I would arrive at 7.30 and prepare the briefing for the senior officers. Primarily, what we had to establish was the aircraft and crew availability for the day, and to see what, if any, shuffling was needed to complete the programme. Occasionally, even this preparation went haywire and we had to play the day by ear, bearing in mind that all TANSOR operations had to fly and that the training programme was essential for the fighter boys as they prepared for detachments and exercises. In all of this it was imperative to give the new boys all the practice that they needed and still appear even handed in the allocations and re-shuffles that took place. Some days I walked a very fine line.

Then there were the briefings at High Wycombe that Tony had to attend from time to time. This was a routine gathering of representatives from all of the UK operational bases that needed the use of the tanker facilities offered by RAF Marham. Although informal, in many ways it was the RAF's way of enabling all the glitches and hold-ups (real or otherwise) in the refuelling operations to be aired, discussed and any lessons learned and shared without rancour and finger pointing. It seemed to work rather well.

There were twenty or so senior officers in attendance, representing the whole of the UK. The Wing Commander in charge used to open the meeting after the regulation coffee and biscuits. He gave an overview of the situation from HQ's perspective, then the chat went round the table. Usually between each report, there was a comment or two from Tony as the Marham spokesman, as almost any air to air refuelling matters inevitably involved the Victors.

Questions were traditionally taken as they arose, so there was no big end-of-meeting question and answer session to endure. It was always a pleasant meeting as there were no 'brownie points' to be earned by anyone, whatever was discussed. By 2.30 pm it was usually over and after a leisurely lunch Tony would head back home to prepare his report of that meeting for the Station Commander the following day. Only occasionally would he ask for a private meeting with the CO on the contents of the report. Usually this would be as a result of a situation that had already arisen, or was about to arise, where simply too much was being asked of the tanker fleet at any one time, and in his view the system was being stretched too far.

Two to three weeks prior to the next MINEVAL, although I did not know it at the time, I received a call from the Station Commander to join him and some of the other senior officers in his office. It wasn't just for coffee and biscuits – we were having a MINEVAL in a couple of weeks and my input was needed. Firstly a date was set; though I'm sure my agreement with the date chosen was hardly a deciding factor. My thoughts on all aspects of the intensive flying and tanking utilisation that it would require, was needed as a component part of the CO's overall plan for the fun and games that were to follow. He then re-confirmed the obvious, that no leaks were allowed and that the clock started counting down from now! As I walked back into my office, I locked all the doors behind me and double-checked all my security procedures.

My previous MINEVAL and TACEVAL experiences started at 3 am on the morning of the exercise, from now on until I left the RAF, they would start at 3 am plus two weeks, and I was still down on the list to take part. However I was in good company, as the Station Commander, who having acknowledged my paperwork that I sent through to the organising team, then advised us that he did not wish to know anything of its contents. As he said, it was a test of the whole station, himself included.

Planning the strengths and deployment of the Victor tankers for any exercise was crucial, but there was a pecking order. For a TACEVAL, it was absolute maximum readiness, with no exceptions whatsoever; for a MINEVAL it was as near to maximum as possible;

and for all other exercises it was the best that could reasonably be achieved with the equipment and manpower available. I still had the TANSOR commitment to fulfil, and of course the training sorties to fly and fulfil for the fighter squadrons. No one was going to thank me for claiming a MINEVAL at Marham as an excuse for not getting a squadron of Phantoms out to Cyprus on detachment because one or two of the new boys on the squadron had not received sufficient practice. Again, it was all a bit of a balancing act and one that no doubt my predecessor, Ernie Wallis, had carried out faultlessly. As I said before, he was a good mentor, but a tough act to follow.

As day one of the MINEVAL approached, I would receive the enquiring phone call from the CO for confirmation that all was ready. At the Friday afternoon meeting in his office we would go over everything in general terms to ensure all the procedures were in place. Only the detail was still unknown. That would unfold the following Monday morning. That 3 am call was not a surprise. Nor was the awaited promotion to Senior Squadron Operations Officer. It was the icing on the cake and elevated my salary to a very comfortable level.

Just after the MINEVAL I returned to RAF Holbeach for the third of my three detachments as temporary Station Commander. The final stay was equally as enjoyable as the first – little wonder the position was never advertised at the local job centre!

With all this experience behind him, it was hardly surprising that the last TACEVAL that Tony was involved with at RAF Marham went faultlessly and both he and the station received a superb report. He was now heading for retirement and his fifty-fifth birthday. In one of the later conversations on that subject with his Station Commander, he had been advised that if he wanted to stay a further three years, then he would receive the CO's full recommendation. During this time he had also attracted the secondary duty of Officer IC Visits. Not in itself an onerous task, but once the novelty of shepherding a group of civilians around the station in the evenings had worn off, it tended to be a bit the same every time, and a further drain on his already limited spare time. All things considered, he believed that he had achieved all that he possibly could in the RAF, and perhaps a little more. It was now time to go. It was one of those natural stages of life that to

Tony was pretty obvious and needed little further thought. The Air Force had been everything he had ever hoped it would be, but it was time to move on and try something new.

By coincidence, Wednesday 8 November 1989 was both his birthday and last day as a serving RAF officer.

CHAPTER 14

Civvy Street and Beyond

It was a really weird feeling to drive out of the gates of RAF Marham for the last time. Sure, I had left the station several times before, heading to another posting, but I always knew there was a pretty sporting chance I would be back. After all, what else can you do with a tanker navigator, other than let him navigate tankers? As that mostly happened from Marham, my eventual return there at some time in the future was hardly going to be a surprise. This time it was different. This time my departure was permanent. My drive home that day was towards my new life in retirement.

Earlier in my time in the RAF, the change of posting from aircrew to 'desk wallah' had been in many ways, in my mind at least, a step down the RAF ladder. If that was really the case, then on that last day at Marham, I stepped off the ladder altogether. I was now for the first time in some thirty years, plain Mr Tony Golds. OK, I had been told I could retain my rank for 'official' purposes and certainly the guys on the gate at Marham always extended officer rank courtesies to me when I visited for golf or other social and sporting functions. They still do for that matter, and I find that extremely agreeable, even after all these years. But truth to tell I was now a real live, 100 per cent, civilian; it was something I had not experienced in my adult life and would mean a whole new way of thinking.

However, before full and total civilianisation set in, I had my leaving 'dos' to attend – all five of them! I had been used to partying

*throughout my RAF career, but these few days took it to new heights,
even for me. There were three farewell bashes at Marham. One
was from the section staff, held in the catering division of the Ops
Centre. The next was with the Operations team and our civilian
staff, and the last was the more formal official bash thrown by the
Station Commander. It was probably put on to ensure I really was
going, as one wag wittily put it. All were brilliant in their own
way, though I probably remember the official one the most, mainly
because of the very nice things that the CO said about me to the
assembled throng. In my response I could not resist commenting
that if he had only taken the time to have written all those nice
things he had just said, in my earlier official 1369s (annual written
report for all commissioned RAF officers covering their career to
date and their promotion prospects) whilst I was a serving officer, I
might well have made Air Vice-Marshal, which would have meant
that I would now be retiring on an Air Vice-Marshal's pension!
That raised a distinct chuckle round the Mess, but the reality was
that I was leaving on an elevated pension of a Squadron Leader. That
would make life for Maryse and me very comfortable, with little to
worry about except how to spend it and what to spend it on next,
whilst enjoying our retirement. I could have no complaints. Indeed,
spending a sizeable chunk of that retirement income on various
holidays was high on our agenda.*

*In the first year or so we headed off on holiday to Paris and then
further south to Monte Carlo where we enjoyed ourselves immensely
in the Mediterranean sun. Because of my past life, it was hardly
surprising that I did have a few restrictions on travel destinations
imposed, at least for the first five years of becoming a civilian. East
European and former communist countries were a real no-no to
visit, and for certain, parts of the Middle East and South America,
especially Iran and Argentina, were not likely to be included on my
cruise list for quite a while, if ever.*

*So we took out our walking boots from the cupboard, dusted
them off, polished them up, and put them back to good use. We went
up north and did some serious walking. We did the coast to coast
walk, following some of the legendary Arthur Wainwright trails,
and spent many enjoyable days exploring the paths across both the
Yorkshire and Derbyshire Dales.*

Sometimes we went for just a week, sometimes for anything up to three weeks. On occasions Janine, Maryse's daughter, and her partner Kevin, joined us on these walking trips. It was a real joy to have them along and to share the pleasure of the open countryside with them. It was also a great chance, usually over dinner in the evening, to catch up on news of family and friends – something that had been in short supply during the aircrew days when I wasn't able to be around as much as I would have wished.

When we were away on our own, Maryse and I paid scant notice to the weather and rarely had any walks called off because conditions were too bad. We had all the correct 'bad weather' clothing and found the kit worked well and kept us warm and dry in all but the severest of conditions. Even when mother nature threw her worst at us, there was nothing much that a hot bath, a couple of gin and tonics and a nice meal would not sort out. As we were both capable map readers (no real surprise there), we had taken to singling out the more remote paths and tracks to follow and thoroughly enjoyed the quiet and peacefulness that it brought. I recall on one occasion, following a light dusting of snow, we retraced our own steps on one path after a four or five-hour walk. Our outward tracks were still the only footprints in the snow to be seen for the whole of the route.

We also walked our way round the Scilly Isles a couple of times. We based ourselves on St Mary's, following my first ever civilian helicopter flight to get there. (I did find it a bit ironic that after all these years as aircrew and over 4,000 hours' airborne, I still managed to find some aviation firsts to accomplish during retirement, as a civilian!)

Having walked every path and lane available on St Mary's during the first day or so, we headed by ferry to Tresco, St Martin's and the other islands to do the same with them. On both visits we were blessed with brilliant weather for the whole time. Over supper one evening, I recall saying to Maryse that I could see why people chose to live there, despite the size and remoteness of the islands. She took the opportunity to remind me how well we were established in Norfolk and how happy we were living there. Point taken.

With increased leisure time available to be spent on the golf course, my handicap went down fairly swiftly and my standard of squash improved greatly, due it has to be said, more to experience *and technique than sheer speed and stamina; though all these sport-ing activities certainly helped me to keep very fit and active.*

It was great that my son John still listed both these sports amongst his interests, and from time to time I was able to enjoy those activities with him. He would win at golf, but I could still beat him at squash.

The course at Marham was my primary golfing venue, though I often received invitations from Ryston, King's Lynn, Middleton and Denver, to add a little variety to my game. The Masonic Golfing Society also had tournaments in the area, and I usually managed to get an entry to most of them. My interest in hockey was continuing well in the veterans' teams and I turned out regularly for clubs in King's Lynn and Norwich. However, I have to confess, that the after-game socialising started to become a bit much. The lure of a nice meal and a Saturday evening out with Maryse made a regular bar session with my team colleagues less of an attractive proposition and slowly it and the hockey began to drop down my order of priorities. Squash, though, stayed high on my list of 'must dos' and I continued to play at both the Downham Market and Upwell clubs on a regular basis, usually on a Friday.

In between all these sporting activities there was a great deal of gardening to do at Boughton. We had the chance to buy an extra acre of land at the back of the house and extend the garden. In fact, it virtually doubled it, allowing us to plant several hundred trees and make a huge lawn out of the remainder. We had already created two ponds (by digging them out by hand ourselves) and were rewarded by an increasing influx of birds and wildlife. To our delight it ranged from the smallest of insects who arrived to inhabit the ponds, to full grown muntjac deer who wandered in from time to time and even included the occasional visiting grass snake. This size of garden was quite a huge undertaking and needed constant attention. I used to prefer to tackle in bite-sized lumps, a couple of hours at a time, stop for a coffee, then do something else for the rest of the day. That way when I returned the next day, I was still pretty keen and enthusiastic. If I spent too long in one go, my keenness tended to get easily drained. Nonetheless, the end result was great and the garden turned out just how I hoped it would. Maryse had her reservations, and still does to this day.

In the run up to this change of his life, Tony had spent many years assimilating himself into the local civic and social scene around Downham Market. Several years earlier he had been introduced to the various organisations involved with charitable fundraising and civic assistance programmes. He liked what he saw and decided to join in. He was a founder member of the Downham Lions and as such also became involved with the teams from the Rotary Club and Round Table. He was an active member in the Lions and helped out on occasions with the other nearby charitable organisations for many years. But it was the local Freemasons Lodge that whetted his appetite the most, and it was the St Winnold Lodge on the corner of London Road and Ryston End in Downham Market that would become his primary interest in that area.

Unsurprisingly, with its close proximity to Marham, and with the run down of the V-bomber force and latterly the Victor tanker force from that airfield, there was a considerable number of ex-aircrew who had reached the end of their flying careers and bought retirement homes in West Norfolk. Downham Market seemed to be a particular favourite area to settle. Equally unsurprisingly was the fact that many of them, like Tony, were attracted to the various civic organisations that the area had to offer. At the Lions, Round Table, Rotary Club and particularly St Winnold Lodge, Tony found himself among friends and like-minded people.

He had joined the lodge way back during his RAF days in 1979. By October 1990 he had worked his way systematically through its various officer posts, following the natural Masonic progression, until in that year he became Worshipful Master of the St Winnold Lodge. He also joined several of the side orders associated with St Winnold and found great interest in the workings and history of this ancient order.

I was very happy with my Masonic life at St Winnold and greatly enjoyed all that it had to offer. It had a regularity and order that I found matched the in-built disciplines that had remained part of me after all those years in the Air Force.

There was a challenge with every new job taken on in the Lodge, and the continuance of the charitable work that I found particularly rewarding and something I felt I needed to do. However, after passing through the chair of St Winnold lodge I was invited to join some of the side orders available to past masters. I found these new avenues all most interesting and decided to expand my Masonic activities and look towards groups and meetings in these other orders through-out Norfolk and the wider East Anglia. By joining these other orders there arose the opportunity to become more involved in their admini-stration and organisation, an activity that with my background, I found easy to cope with.

On occasions, I found that I was required to present lectures, usually on historical matters, which required an amount of research and preparation, somewhat akin to my report presentations in the RAF. I felt quite at home doing this and with more of the same spreading out in front of me, life in retirement was really becoming comfortable, full and rewarding – I had scarcely a dull moment.

Whilst still retaining strong links with St Winnold Lodge, Tony's Masonic interests had now expanded to cover over twenty-five other orders. This array of commitments kept him both interested and busy. Usually, he would attend three meetings a week, which worked out at two during the weekday evenings and one at the weekend. He was getting invitations from all over the country and even some from abroad. He happily accepted UK invitations and some from France, but the ones from countries as far away as India were just a bit too much of a distance for even a couple of meetings. By the mid to late 1990s the procession of invitations had become a flood and out of sheer practicality he was only able to accept about one in three that dropped through the letterbox. He could well have been out every night of the week and easily doubled the mileage that his Volvo was putting on the clock.

By chance, his home at Boughton was almost under the Marham circuit. With that and his continued attendance at the station for golf and other occasional social functions, Tony had kept him-self abreast of the broader picture at his old station. He was able to see for himself the passing of the Victor tanker into RAF and aviation history. He also saw the evolution of the station into a predominantly Tornado base, with only the venerable Canberras from 39 Squadron for company, as they served out the last of their operational days through to June 2006 in a reconnaissance role.

With a generous percentage of the local population and quite a number of his circle of friends and acquaintances made up of ex-aircrew and ex-RAF types, there was always the opportunity to talk through this evolution and change at his old station with his contemporaries. They all had similar backgrounds and experiences and produced some lively discussions from time to time. It also helped to pass the odd hour or two over a pint after squash, or between courses at the monthly Lodge dinners.

Life in retirement was not all outdoors and energetic. Maryse and I enjoyed fairly frequent trips to London to the theatre, to the ballet, and to the various musicals running in the West End. Sometimes we went on our own and other times with like-minded friends. Frequently, we stayed at the RAF Club in Piccadilly. It was central for most of London and suited us perfectly. We were always looked after well, although once, following a mix-up over a double booking, we were reallocated rooms at the Calvary Club, which by chance was situated immediately next door. The ambience there was really superb and a step up from the RAF Club. It had a level of service that we felt would be hard to match anywhere but in the very top echelons of the London hotel trade. Sadly, in all our years of visiting, that was the only time the RAF Club messed up – more's the pity.

Back at home, John and I went to most of the Ipswich Town Football Club home fixtures. Although Norwich was equally as close for travelling, we never were attached to Norwich City and only visited Carrow Road for the local derbies. John was really a Leeds United fan, but distance was a significant problem in getting him to their home games. Ipswich, however, was convenient, even though I never could convert him to becoming a real Ipswich supporter.

For home matches we used to leave Boughton mid-morning and drive to the home of the mother of a good friend of mine, Brian Rogers. We would then stop to have a cup of tea with her, leave the car at her house and walk to the match. After it was over, we had a quick pint at one of the nearby pubs, wandered back to Brian's mum's place, nattering on about how good or bad the match had been, have another cup of tea and a sticky bun, and then head for home. To me, that seemed a most civilised and agreeable way of attending a football match that could hardly be bettered.

Maryse and I had occasionally managed to get all the children together. It was great to see John, Piers, Janine and Lisa all together relaxing at the house in Boughton. Regretfully, we have never managed to get all the children and all the grandchildren together in the same way. They have visited on many occasions, but in more discrete family units. The pressures of coordinating four children, five grandchildren and their assorted commitments to schools, sports, pets and all their other social activities, has always proved a logistical impossibility. Come to think of it, it may be a blessing in disguise. I'm not sure I could cope with such an influx of numbers in one hit, into our more regulated life. I prefer to have the ability to talk to one person at a time. Trying to hold a series of simultaneous conversations with two or three young children at the same time, as seems to be needed with lively youngsters these days, is perhaps an art I no longer feel I have. In smaller numbers I am able to talk, play and enjoy their company, and then when they have returned home, bask in the quietness that has returned to our home. On these occasions I frequently contemplate how their lives will pan out for them. I hope it is as good for them as mine has been for me.

Having spent most of my adult life as aircrew, one of the things I always wanted to find out was if I had what it took to be a pilot. One year Maryse bought me a lesson at Norwich Airport for a present. I struggled mightily with the first hour or so in the little Cessna, but the subsequent lessons went OK and I started to both make sense of what I was supposed to be doing and to get a glimpse of the enjoyment that most RAF pilots had obviously seen in flying. After the appropriate number of lessons and passing the many ground and airborne CAA (Civil Aviation Authority) tests needed for a Private Pilot's licence, I too, joined the ranks of the likes of Banfy, Jeremy, Dick, and Gus, and became a pilot. It gave me a healthy insight into the world as they must have seen it. However, it was a rather expensive solo hobby and one that Maryse did not want to share. After a while, it would have to be abandoned in favour of continuing golf, squash, walking and my other time-consuming interests. I was delighted that I had put in the effort and achieved my wings, albeit I had left it rather late!

All in all, as I mentioned earlier, my life in the RAF had turned out exactly as I had hoped it would. Now in retirement, the second phase of my life, with Maryse, our children, grandchildren and my Masonic duties, was turning out just as well ... Not too bad for an evacuee with just two 'O' Levels.

Aircraft Flown

Training and Operational
- Vickers Valetta
- Vickers Varsity
- Gloucester Meteor NF
- English Electric Canberra T4
- English Electric Canberra B2
- English Electric Canberra B15
- Vickers Valiant (Tanker)
- Handley-Page Victor 1A (Tanker)
- Handley-Page Victor 2 (Tanker)
- British Aerospace Dominie

Others
- Douglas DC3
- Avro Anson
- Martin B 57
- Piper 'Scout'
- Blackburn Beverley
- Bristol Argosy
- Avro Lincoln
- Avro Shackleton

Civilian
- Cessna 152

APPENDIX 2

Units

- Topcliffe
- Lindholme
- Bassingbourn
- Tengah
- Gaydon
- Finningley
- Marham
- Brampton
- Cirencester
- Holbeach

Air to Air Refuelling Operations

Feeder Plane
- Valiant to Valiant
- Valiant to Vulcan
- Valiant to Javelin
- Valiant to Lightning
- Valiant to Victor

- Victor to Victor
- Victor to Vulcan
- Victor to Nimrod
- Victor to Hercules C130
- Victor to Lightning
- Victor to Jaguar
- Victor to Buccaneer
- Victor to Phantom
- Victor to Harrier
- Victor to Tornado

Receiver Plane
- Victor to Victor

RAF Air to Air Refuelling Procedure Diagrams

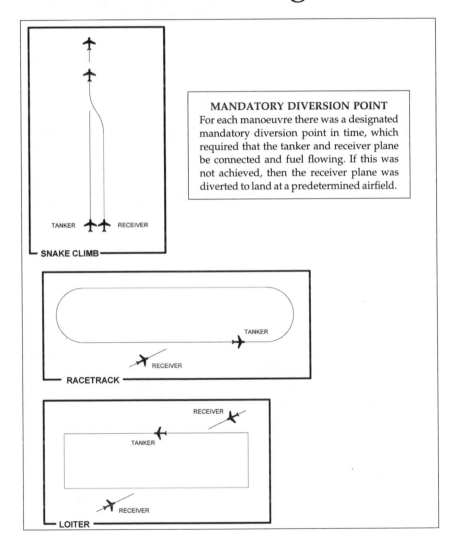

MANDATORY DIVERSION POINT
For each manoeuvre there was a designated mandatory diversion point in time, which required that the tanker and receiver plane be connected and fuel flowing. If this was not achieved, then the receiver plane was diverted to land at a predetermined airfield.

TANKER   RECEIVER

SNAKE CLIMB

TANKER

RECEIVER

RACETRACK

RECEIVER

TANKER

RECEIVER

LOITER

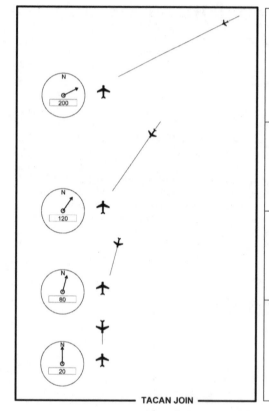

Receiver aircraft at FL280, 200 miles to run, approximately 45° to starboard. Tanker at FL300.

Tanker RT
'Tanker to receiver. Confirm FL280. Channel selection 40 air to air. Make heading 220.'

Receiver aircraft maintains FL280, 120 miles to run, approximately 35° to starboard. Tanker maintains FL300.

Tanker RT
'Tanker to receiver make heading 200.'

Receiver aircraft maintains FL280, 80 miles to run, approximately 15° to starboard. Tanker maintains FL300.

Tanker RT
'Tanker to receiver make heading 185.'

Receiver aircraft starts to climb to FL300, 20 miles to run. Both aircraft on reciprocal headings. Tanker maintains FL300.

Tanker RT
'Tanker to receiver make heading 180.'

TACAN JOIN

The standard procedures used by the RAF to ensure tanker and receiver planes met up according to schedule.

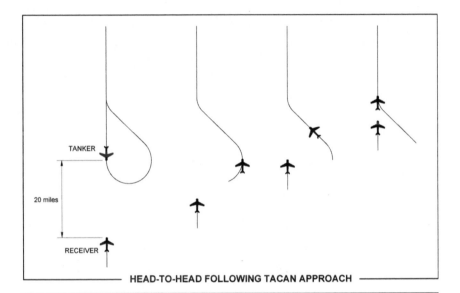

TANKER

20 miles

RECEIVER

HEAD-TO-HEAD FOLLOWING TACAN APPROACH

HEAD-TO-HEAD – INITIAL TACAN APPROACH

For the head-to-head procedure the TACAN is used to position the fast closing aircraft (1,000 mph closing speed).

The Nav/Plotter's TACAN instrument reads off the distance between the tanker and the receiver aircraft and indicates an angular deflection from the tanker nose. He then 'talks' the receiver plane into the twenty mile position with instructions to both pilots.

The procedural join as shown in the diagram then follows, starting with the tanker commencing a broad turn to take it back in a reciprocal heading. This initial part of the turn presents the incoming receiver plane with a large side profile of the tanker for identification and location purposes for the visual join.

Index

179